A Boy Named Red

A TRUE CRIME STORY

Richard Rashke

AUTHOR OF
THE KILLING OF KAREN SILKWOOD

Red Rabbit Books

Published by Red Rabbit Books
Editorial.Team@RedRabbit-Books.com

Book Cover Design & Interior Layout by Scribeworks, LLC.

Originally published in 2023 by Red Rabbit Books

A Boy Named Red/ Richard Rashke—paperback edition, 2024
ISBN 979-8-8693-4044-3

OTHER BOOKS BY RICHARD RASHKE

Nonfiction

The Killing of Karen Silkwood
Escape From Sobibor
Stormy Genius
Capitol Hill in Black and White
Runaway Father
Trust Me
Useful Enemies
The Whistleblower's Dilemma
Children's Letters to A Holocaust Survivor: "Dear Esther"

Plays

Dear Esther
Season To Season

For Red

To Guy and Bruce

TABLE OF CONTENTS

INTRODUCTION...i

THE NARRATIVE 1

    PARADISE LOST...3

THE ANALYSIS 65

    THE TOUGH QUESTIONS...67

    THE MAKING OF ALPHONSE HORNE 71

    THE MISFIT 79

    ON THE LOOSE 81

    HIDING ALPHONSE 83

    ERASING ALPHONSE 89

DODGE BALL...93

    THE PARTING OF THE VEIL 95

    THE SHUFFLE AND THE SHELF....................................99

    A VIEW FROM THE TOP...103

    NEED-TO-KNOW 105

ABUSING THE POWER 109

    THE BOY WHO KNEW TOO MUCH 111

    THE BOY WHO SAW TOO MUCH.................................121

    HOUNDING HARTE 125

    THE GAMBLE...131

THE SYSTEMIC FLAW 135

FILLING HOLES 137

MISSION IMPOSSIBLE 143

THE ONE-DAY INVESTIGATION 149

JAMES VOSS 151

DR. ROSS BAKER..155

DETECTIVE WERNER VOEGELI.................................163

SHERIFF JOSEPH DORR 171

CONCLUSIONS...175

WALWORTH COUNTY...177

THE CRIMINAL COVER UP 181

SUICIDE...183

SUICIDE—A SECOND LOOK 187

HOMICIDE? 189

JUSTICE FOR RED 193

AFTERWORD 195

ACKNOWLEDGMENTS...197

CHAPTER END NOTES..199

ABOUT THE AUTHOR 205

INTRODUCTION

Early in 2020, I received a phone call from an alumnus of Divine Word Seminary in East Troy, Wisconsin. The caller had entered the school in the fall of 1960, six months after the tragic death of Kenneth "Red" Rudnitski. Sixty years later, the caller was still troubled by the unanswered questions surrounding Red's death.

The reason the caller sought me out was because I too was an East Troy alumnus. I had graduated from the seminary high school in 1953. Ordained a priest in 1963—three years after Red's death—I was assigned to another high school seminary as a teacher and Assistant Prefect (dean of students) and served in that job for five years. I resigned from the priesthood in 1975 and became a writer.

The caller's story intrigued me. The more he told me about Red's death, the more the pieces didn't seem to fit. When he suggested I write a book about this icy cold case, I agreed.

Some associates questioned my decision to re-open the Kenneth "Red" Rudnitski case. It's 60 years old, they reminded me. Why exhume the boy's ghost, they asked? No one cares, they said. Let the boy rest in peace, they argued. *Cui bono* they asked?

If what I knew of *A Boy Named Red* was even partly true, Red was not resting in peace and never would until the truth was unraveled—if it ever could be. My plan was simple: Give that fifteen-year-old boy a voice; redeem his name; if crimes have been committed against him, hold the criminals accountable; and offer Red a belated measure of justice.

***

No stranger to cold cases, I understood the unique problems and pitfalls I would have to face if I chose to poke around the edges of the story. My true-story World War II book *Escape From Sobibor* took place in 1943. My true story cold-case thriller, *The Killing of Karen Silkwood*, took place in the mid-1970s. No one had to tell me that

I would be navigating through the dense fog of fuzzy memories and a mine field of contradictions and lies. Above all, I recognized that it might not be possible to find truth after sixty years of dust and mildew and that I might end up alone in a blind alley.

What ultimately convinced me to take the risk and to investigate Red's tragic death was a precious asset. Many of Red's classmates and fellow students, now in their mid to late seventies, were willing to guide me. With their help, I managed to find and interview or contact more than thirty of the 106 students attending the Seminary in 1960. They combed and sifted through old memories. They opened their hearts with courage. Some memories were mere shadows on the wall of time. Some events were either forgotten, only partially remembered, or buried so deeply that they could not be reached. Some have scars, relics of questions still unanswered. Others have stubborn wounds that refuse to heal. In the end, each offered recollections that helped me stitch the tragic death of Red Rudnitski into a coherent whole, albeit with gaps.

I feel compelled to point out that, with few exceptions, the former 1960 students at the East Troy seminary high school viewed their training as an enriching experience; they spoke about their time there critically but with fondness; and they felt indebted for the training and education they received.

In my search to exhume truth, I had invaluable assistance from a former Divine Word Seminary student Dick Hahner. His experience, contacts, investigation skills, and critiques of work-in-progress were indispensable. A Bronze-Star Vietnam War Veteran, Mr. Hahner spent thirty-three years as a U.S. Department of Justice criminal investigator. As I, Hahner believes that the death of a 15-year-old-boy mattered in 1960 and still matters today.

***

Puzzling the sixty-year-old death of a boy in a Catholic high school seminary is a sensitive topic that demands clear and careful treatment. Consequently, I have divided *A Boy Named Red* into three sections:

An objective journalistic rendering of the story based on interviews with attribution and documentation.

A contextual and historical analysis of the evidence, contradictions, and gaps in the journalistic rendering.

A series of conclusions based on the facts of the case, logic, and observations of professionals—doctors, lawyers, criminal and forensic investigators, and mental health professionals.

THE NARRATIVE

PARADISE LOST

Divine Word Seminary in East Troy, Wisconsin, thirty-five miles southwest of Milwaukee, was a paradise, especially for boys who grew up on asphalt metropolises of Milwaukee and Chicago. The brick school building sat on a bluff overlooking lower Lake Beulah which sparkled like a silver coin in the sun. Most of the houses on the lower lake were summer cottages, set back from the shore and shaded by oak, maple, and chestnut trees. Motor boating and water skiing took place mainly on the larger upper lake.

A Bud May Photo.

Upper and lower Lake Beulah were linked by a shallow channel dotted with tree stumps poking out of the water like gravestones. The water was so clear that if you stood still, you could count your toes. The Beulahs were widely known for their bluegill, sunfish, perch, and bass hiding in the cattails and lily pads along the shoreline.

The high school seminary sat on 170 acres—part farm, part lakefront, part wasteland. The missionary religious order that staffed the seminary purchased this slice of bucolic paradise for $27,000. The school opened in 1936, a home-away-from-home for 100 high school students wanting to become missionary priests who made a difference. The new seminary was deemed such an important contribution to the Church and to East Troy Township that Milwaukee Archbishop Samuel Stritch graced the first graduation with his presence.

Divine Word Seminary was hidden from the world about four miles from the unincorporated town of East Troy. As you left the county highway and drove onto St. Peter's Road, leading to the seminary, you passed through the school farm with grazing black and white Holsteins and fields of alfalfa, hay, and corn. On the other side of the road a dense hedge shielded the seminary from its neighbors.

Behind the seminary, across a field and down a hill was tiny Army Lake. Compared to Beulah, which reached a depth of almost sixty feet, Army Lake was shallow and froze in November long before its neighbor. The students played hockey along Army Lake's shoreline while the center was still open water. The bottom of the lake was littered with hockey pucks.

When the seminary Prefect thought Beulah was safe enough for skating and hockey, he would head for the boathouse with an ax. The whole student body would follow in anticipation. The Prefect would walk down the white steel pier iced in place and carefully step on to the ice. Then he would cut a hole with the ax and measure the thickness of the ice. If he thought it was safe for skating, he would give the thumbs up and the students would let out a cheer as loud as a stadium full of Green Bay Packer fans.

Frozen Lake Beulah. A Dick Hahner Photo.

The students would then tote their two hockey cages from Army Lake and set them on the ice near the boathouse. Then they would impatiently wait for the rest of the lake to turn into glass. Before snow covered it, they would skate for miles. Every now and then, gliding over the shallow channel, they would see a muskrat under the ice, swimming back home to the safety of its mound.

Directly behind the seminary was a meadow shaped like a bowl. If you sat quietly in its grasses, you could watch goldfinches flit, count Red-Shafted Flickers darting from tree to tree, and smile at the Killdeer running in nervous spurts up and down the dirt track that cut through the meadow, hoping you would go away. Half way down from the lip of the bowl was a rickety wood ski jump. Very few students dared to fly over the road and land, more or less safely, on the unpacked snow.

As you stood on the bluff outside the school building above Lake Beulah, there was a path to the right that followed the lake's shoreline and led to the "point." Looking down from the point above the path, you could see the entire lower Lake Beulah, part of the upper lake, and the swamp that hemmed half of the seminary property.

A Bud May Photo.

Dressed in delicate shades of brown that came alive when the wind rippled its grasses, the swamp had an aura of primitive beauty. It was filled with muskrat mounds and beaten trails that the furry rats shared with raccoons and mink. Red-wing black birds squawked from reeds. If you were quiet, you could hear a pheasant call or see a great blue heron fishing on one leg in the fresh water at the edge of the swamp. In the middle of the wasteland was an island covered with trees, a relic of the woods of yesteryear. If you carefully picked your way bog-to-bog, you could walk there. And, when you stood on top of the island hill, you felt like you were the first person to have ever set foot on it.

On March 8, 1960, the Divine Word paradise turned into a nightmare. But, to give some context, we will begin in early February.

Early February 1960

Thirteen-year-old Tim Fitzgerald was enlarging and printing photos in the seminary darkroom. He was a freshman and described himself as a vulnerable "pretty boy," shy and somewhat withdrawn. After Tim's father abandoned the family, Tim's mother was unable to support her six children and sought help from the parish priest. According to Mr. Fitzgerald, the priest advised Anne Veronica to give her son to Chicago's Angel Guardian Orphanage where he would be safe and receive a good education. As a ward of the state of Illinois in a Wisconsin boarding school with students who had parents and a family, Tim felt "different." While the other students went home during vacations, he went back to Angel Guardian and the German nuns who reared him.

For Tim, photography was more than just a hobby. The darkroom was a place where, as Mr. Fitzgerald put it, he "came alive." Before long, he was better than good with a lens, developing pans, and an enlarger. As the 1960 seminary yearbook *Spokesman* described him:

"Tim is a regular shutter bug and is often seen with a camera cocked and ready for a shot. He rarely misses a chance to show his stuff with a camera at any sporting event or play production. 'Fitzy' almost ranks with professionals."

The seminary basement darkroom was almost as professional as the photographer Tim Fitzgerald. The small room, six-feet by six-feet, was fully equipped with two enlargers, a sink with running water, two developing pans, a red developing light, and a shelf with a row of photo chemicals, each neatly labeled. A string stretched across the work area where newly developed photographs could hang and dry. A thick, light-proof curtain separated the work area from the rest of the room which didn't have a door opening into the basement corridor. To enter and leave, student photographers like Tim had to pass through the janitorial/paint room. That space was the domain of Brother Alphonse Horne.

Tim Fitzgerald heard a rap on the darkroom door that February morning in 1960. Expecting his classmate Teddy Brown, a fellow photographer who had stepped out to run an errand, Tim called out "Yes!" It was a darkroom code for—it's okay to enter without exposing film under development.

Brother Alphonse parted the curtain and entered. Without saying a word, he grabbed Tim by the shoulder, spun him around, and slammed him against the wall. A 30-year-old World War II veteran trained in hand-to-hand combat, Brother Alphonse was a short stocky man with large hands and the body of a wrestler. Tim weighed just a smidgen over one hundred pounds, and his right hand was bandaged because he had cut it on a table saw the week before. "It was so sore," Mr. Fitzgerald recalled, "I couldn't use it to even adjust the focus on the enlarger."

Brother Alphonse pressed so tightly against Tim that he could feel Alphonse's erection. And when Alphonse grabbed one of Tim's arms in a hammer lock and shoved his other hand into Alphonse's crotch, Tim knew what was about to happen. As Mr. Fitzgerald recalled, he was too shocked and scared to cry out.

Before Brother Alphonse could bend Tim over the darkroom counter and rape him, there was another rap on the door. "Yes!" Tim called out. It was Teddy Brown. As soon as Brown entered the darkroom, Alphonse released Tim, parted the curtain, brushed past Brown, and walked out of the darkroom without a word.

Tim did not report the attack to his Prefects, Fathers Paul Jacobi and John McHenry, because he didn't trust them. Mr. Fitzgerald said he felt ashamed, feared reprisals, and he did not think the Prefects would take him seriously.

It is important to point out that Tim Fitzgerald's response to the sexual assault was typical. Researchers have learned that child sex abuse is one of the most under-reported crimes in the United States; only 12% of those attacked report the crime. According to the Rape, Abuse, Incest National Network, a child is sexually abused every nine minutes. There are many reasons why the crime is so under reported, among which are: shame, fear of reprisals, fear of not being believed, too traumatized to report the crime. Authorities frequently accuse the boys who report the crime "of taking things too seriously."

Tim Fitzgerald age 19.

After the assault, Brother Alphonse began stalking Tim Fitzgerald. "I avoided him as best I could," Mr. Fitzgerald recalled. "When I needed to go to the basement, I made sure someone was with me. If I couldn't find anyone and saw Alphonse sweeping or mopping, I would turn around and hurry back up the stairs. I never went back into the darkroom alone. It terrified me."

Besides being a good photographer, Tim Fitzgerald was also a dedicated athlete who engaged in every competitive sport Angel Guardian had to offer. Baseball and track were his favorites. Tim took to running, even though it was winter and the grounds were frequently covered with ice and snow. Sometimes he sprinted around the cinder track behind the school building. Sometimes he ran down St. Peter's road that fed into the local county highway leading to the town of East Troy.

Running made Tim feel safe and secure. It was a brief respite from the constant anxiety that gnawed on him since the assault. He was living in a boarding school with a sexual predator stalking him. Would Brother Alphonse attack again? Where? When? This time would he kill? With no one to talk to but two Prefects whom he didn't trust, 13-year-old Tim bore his secret alone. It was gnawing at his young masculinity, his self-identity, and his self-confidence.

***

Although it was a devastating shock to be assaulted by a religious brother in a Catholic high school seminary, it didn't come as a complete surprise to Tim Fitzgerald. A Chicago city boy, he loved to work on the school's dairy and hog farm, with its fields of hay, corn, and alfalfa. Brothers Felix Lammers and Conrad Schmidt ran the farm. Brother Felix was a tall, lean, straight-talking John Wayne type. Brother Conrad was beefy and silent with a big heart.

Tim mucked out barns, fed pigs, collected baskets of fallen apples for their dessert, prepped cows for milking, and helped Felix dress the hogs he routinely slaughtered to feed more than a hundred students and the faculty. Brother Felix soon became a strong and kind father figure.

One day, Brother Felix called Tim aside and warned him: "If you have any concerns about Alphonse, come see me." Mr. Fitzgerald said that he is convinced that Brother Felix didn't know Brother Alphonse was an *active* pedophile, he only suspected it.

"If Felix had known," Mr. Fitzgerald said, "he would have done something about it."

Brother Felix gave the same warning to Red's classmate Dick Hahner. A Chicago city boy like Fitzgerald, Hahner loved working on the farm and spent as much time there as he could. He began by mucking out the barns and soon graduated to spreading the manure on the fields in a small Ford tractor. Brother Felix trusted Hahner so much that he taught the boy how to handle the large John Deere and haul silage. Sitting high up on the tractor was both a thrill and a responsibility that Hahner never forgot.

"Brother Felix and Brother Conrad showed an obvious dislike for Alphonse," Mr. Hahner recalled as he talked about his days working on the farm. "Felix cautioned me to avoid Alphonse."

Brother Jude Heeks gave the same advice to Red's classmate Harry May, who was also a photographer. Jude was the seminary office manager, organist, and amateur ham radio operator. Besides his upstairs office in the faculty quarters, Brother Jude had a room in the basement not far from the darkroom. The room doubled as his broadcast studio and the pick-up and drop-off station for students who sent their soiled clothes to a laundry in East Troy. Former East Troy students described Brother Jude as warm, caring, ever smiling, and friendly—but not overly friendly—and "everybody's favorite."

Like Brother Felix, Brother Jude warned Harry May to keep away from Brother Alphonse. "I did," Mr. May said. "Whenever I was in the darkroom, it was always with someone else."

Other former student photographers Greg Laka and Marty Koleno confirmed that Brother Alphonse liked to hang around the darkroom. Mr. Laka remembered another student telling him that Brother Alphonse had gotten "too close to him" in the darkroom, but he couldn't recall the student's name. Mr. Laka said it could have been Tim Fitzgerald, but he wasn't sure. Mr. Koleno also recalled being warned to be careful around Brother Alphonse.

Mid-February 1960

Bill Burrows was *more* than suspicious of Brother Alphonse. A seminary junior, Burrows recalled that one day in February 1960, he was sitting on the floor of the empty infirmary replacing an electric outlet during an after-lunch work period. Burrows was handy with tools, something he had learned from his father. The infirmary was isolated. While Burrows was fiddling with the outlet, Brother Alphonse crept up behind him.

Bill Burrows

"He put his hands on my shoulders," Mr. Burrows recalled, "and began scratching and massaging my back. I was very uncomfortable with it. I stood up, turned to Alphonse and glowered, saying something like 'What do you want?' Embarrassed, Alphonse turned away."

Bill Burrows told his friend Ed Harte what had happened. "He was upset and disturbed," Mr. Harte recalled. "He was shaking. And he was proud of standing up to Alphonse."

Like Tim Fitzgerald, Burrows did not report Brother Alphonse to his Prefects, but for a different reason. Although he was more than annoyed, Mr. Burrows said that he was sexually naive at the time and didn't make much of the advance which criminal prosecutors define as child molestation and mental health professionals call "hot" touching.

Research supports Burrows' admission of sexual naivety. As one researcher put it: "Some boys don't even recognize that they've been sexually assaulted."

Monday March 7th

Lights Out

On Monday night, March 7, 1960, Tim Fitzgerald was restless in his cot in the underclassmen's dormitory on the third floor. It was a huge room with about sixty beds lined up with mathematical precision into three rows, two beds deep. The boys slept head-to-head. Mr. Fitzgerald recalled that a nameless anxiety and fear of Brother Alphonse made it difficult for him to fall asleep after lights out at 8:45. He was terrified that Brother Alphonse would sneak up on him when he finally fell asleep and smother him with a pillow or choke him to death.

Tim's bed was the second in his row, the closest one to the double wooden door with a glowing red exit sign above it. The door opened onto a spotless hallway. To the right of the dorm door was a stairway leading down to the basement. At the end of the hallway was a companion door that opened into the faculty quarters. To the left was a bathroom. Around ten o'clock, a little more than an hour after lights out, Tim saw Kenny "Red" Rudnitski get out of bed and head for the bathroom.

***

Red was a big kid with a medium build, measuring nearly six-feet tall. He played on the junior varsity basketball team with Greg Laka and Bob Kairis and showered after practice. As the 1959 yearbook described Kenny: "'Red' as we called Kenneth Rudnitski because of his curly red locks comes from one of the largest families in our class [eight brothers and three sisters]. He's not the greatest bookworm there ever was, but if you get him on some tough Biology exam, he's all know-how. Red loves all the sports we have here but specializes in basketball."

Red's former classmates described him as a complex teenager and hard to understand. On the one hand, he was likable, fun loving, with a good sense of humor, easy to be around. On the other hand, he was reserved and reluctant to open up. Even his friends never knew what he was thinking or feeling.

"He was a bit of a loner," Mr. Kairis recalled. "He never talked about himself. I accepted it. He was a vibrant kid."

Besides sports, Red played cornet in the school orchestra. Red's coach, Marty Koleno, described him as a good musician, average but dedicated. Koleno sensed that Kenny didn't have a lot of self-confidence. "I tried to make him comfortable," Mr. Koleno recalled.

Red loved the outdoors—walking through the woods, fields, down to Army Lake, strolling the path along the lake shore and the swamp with his friend, Ed Harte. "Red carried a slingshot," Mr. Harte recalled, "but he wouldn't kill anything."

During summer vacation, Red worked at Mercy Hospital in his hometown of Janesville, Wisconsin. If he found it hard to take the life of a blue jay or a squirrel just for fun, he didn't hesitate to shoot the gophers that tunneled into the seminary lawn.

If Red had a flaw other than keeping his feelings and thoughts to himself, it was his temper which flared up during his favorite competitive sports of basketball and handball. Mike Walsh, who was a freshman in 1960 and is a psychologist, described Kenny's temper as an "anger management problem."

Red's close friend Bruce LaMontaigne, who has a degree in social work and has spent his professional life as a counselor, never saw Red angry but he did note an apparent insecurity. "[Kenny] was a roller coaster, up and down," Mr. LaMontaigne recalled. "He didn't fit in...He did not have a good self-image...He was troubled by something. He was the kind of person a pedophile would target."

***

As Divine Word Seminary Head Prefect Father Paul Jacobi would later tell the police, Red was suffering from eye pain. Unable to find a physical cause, the doctor prescribed aspirin to be taken as needed. Red was on his way to the bathroom to take a pill that Monday night March 7th. His eyes were watering so he brought a handkerchief with him to dab them. The police would later find both the aspirin tablet and the handkerchief in the bathroom.

The following account is based on interviews with Mr. Fitzgerald.

Red pushed open the swinging doors under the red exit sign and walked out of the dorm. Although Tim thought it was "strange" that Red had to relieve himself so soon after lights out, he didn't make much of it. But when Red didn't return after ten minutes or so, Tim got up and walked barefoot on the cold floor through the double door. Then he turned and entered the bathroom. The automatic door stopper made no sound when he opened it.

The overhead bathroom lights were off; a night-light dimly lit the room. There was a row of sinks and mirrors along the right wall. On the left side, there was a row of urinals and four gray metal stalls. As soon as Tim entered the bathroom and before the door swished closed, he heard muffled sounds coming from the second stall, the only one with a closed door. Mr. Fitzgerald found it hard to describe what he had heard that March night in 1960 and still hears sixty years later: "Two voices. Heavy breathing. It sounded like someone stifling a laugh. Or someone trying to say something but couldn't."

The laughing, mumbling, snuffling ended moments after the click and swish of the automatic door stopper. The bathroom became as quiet as the March night. Tim padded into the first stall, locked the door, and sat on the toilet seat, listening for voices, sounds of shuffling feet, or breathing. After his eyes adjusted to the dim lighting, Tim stooped and peeked under the separation wall which gave him only a twelve-inch window. He saw two pairs of toe-to-toe feet. One pair was very close to the door and pointing towards the toilet. The feet were bare. The second pair was larger and covered. Mr. Fitzgerald said that the second pair could not have been those of a lowerclassman. No one had left the dormitory after lights-out except Red Rudnitski.

Mr. Fitzgerald made it very clear that he didn't see anything else in the next stall when he peeked under the partition. To get a broader and deeper look, he would have had to lie flat on his stomach and rest his face on the terrazzo floor. Certain that it was Brother Alphonse in the stall with Red, Tim was too scared to risk a second look. If he did, Brother Alphonse might see his face.

Tim's first thought was that Brother Alphonse had Red pinned to the door just as he had pinned him to the wall of the darkroom a month earlier. Only a metal panel separated him from the sexual predator. And Tim knew that Brother Alphonse still considered him a piece of unfinished business.

"I panicked," Mr. Fitzgerald recalled. "All I could think of was to run. It was pure instinct. I sensed danger and fled."

Back in his bed, Tim Fitzgerald waited for Red to return to the dorm. It was a long wait and Tim eventually grew drowsy and fell asleep.

***

Ed Harte was sound asleep a few beds away from Red's cot when something woke him up. It was late at night on March 7th. Harte didn't have a wristwatch and there was no wall clock in the lowerclassmen's dormitory, so he didn't know the exact time.

The 1960 school yearbook described 16-year-old Ed Harte as "an all-around man in sports, studies, and the activities." Although he was only a sophomore, he played first-string guard on the seminary's varsity basketball team. In the classroom, he excelled in Latin and German.

Mr. Harte was choked up when he described what he had seen in the dormitory that March night after Tim Fitzgerald had discovered Red in the bathroom stall with another person whom he believed was Brother Alphonse. It sounded as if Mr. Harte, now in his mid-seventies, was crying as we spoke on the phone.

The following account is based entirely on interviews with Mr. Harte.

Red was on the bed curled in a fetal position. His face was pressed into the mattress. He was shaking and sobbing. Brother Alphonse was sitting on the bed next to Red, pinning him down. Alphonse's face was close to Red's as if he was whispering something into Red's ear. Although Alphonse didn't wear glasses while working, he was wearing a pair of glasses with thick concave lenses that night.

"Alphonse was looking straight at me," Harte recalled. "I still see those glasses with the thick lenses."

Mr. Harte repeated several times during two long interviews that he had faced off with Brother Alphonse before the night of March 7th. "I don't recall what he said," Mr. Harte said. "He upset me and I blew him off. Told him to back off and leave me alone." Mr. Harte also said that he had seen Brother Alphonse hitting on other lowerclassmen, including Red.

Ed Harte

When Brother Alphonse saw Harte staring at him, he released his hold. Red leaped off the bed and ran down the aisle barefoot and sobbing and through the double exit door. Brother Alphonse jumped up from the bed and ran behind Red. The whole scene unfolded in a matter of seconds. Harte watched in silence. Mental health professionals define three basic responses to a trauma—fight, flee, freeze. Red fled. Harte froze.

Like Tim Fitzgerald and Bill Burrows, Ed Harte didn't report Brother Alphonse's attack on Red either to the school's Head Prefect

Father Jacobi or to his assistant Father John McHenry. Mr. Harte said he didn't trust either of them.

Tuesday March 8th

Early Morning

After the six o'clock bell jarred him awake the next morning, Tim Fitzgerald joined the rush to the bathroom to secure a urinal and a sink. As he brushed his teeth in front of the mirror, he noticed that the bare feet in the second bathroom stall were still planted on the floor and pointing toward the toilet, exactly as he had seen them during the night.

Mr. Fitzgerald said that although he thought it was "bizarre," it had never crossed his 13-year-old mind that something may have happened to Red. He said he was still in deep shock over Brother Alphonse's assault and was struggling with the confusing emotions of shame, guilt, and anxiety. What he had witnessed and heard the previous night terrified him so much, Mr. Fitzgerald recalled, that he could not think straight. A pair of bare feet in a bathroom stall was the least of his concerns the next morning.

After he made his bed, Tim joined the other students for Mass, followed by breakfast at seven in the basement refectory. During breakfast, it became clear to the students that something had happened to Kenny. "Red was missing," Mr. Hahner recalled. "His chair at the eight-man table was empty. A quiet settled over the refectory."

One of the boys, who noted Kenny was missing, got up to talk to Father Jacobi who was supervising breakfast from his table perched on a platform. The student told the Head Prefect that he had stopped in the bathroom after mass—just before breakfast—and saw a pair of bare feet in stall number two. He thought it was odd. So did Father Jacobi who immediately went over to Red's table.

"Did anybody see Kenny this morning?" he asked the seven students sitting there.

When the boys said they hadn't, Father Jacobi told Pat Beckman to check the dormitory to see if Kenny was there. As Beckman pushed back his chair, so did Duane Richter and Larry Shadegg. The three boys regularly hung out with Red and were worried about him. *The above and following account is based on independent interviews with Beckman and Richter.* Larry Shadegg is deceased.

***

Beckman, Richter, and Shadegg took the stairs two at a time from the basement to the third floor dormitory which was empty. Then they checked the bathroom and saw the closed stall door and a pair of bare feet. Beckman bent down and peeked under the door which offered a wider and broader view than the partition. It was a shattering moment for the 15-year-old boy. His last memory of Red was laughing and joking while pitching pennies in front of the school the previous afternoon.

"His feet were bluish," Mr. Beckman recalled. "He was just hanging there. I was queasy."

Pat Beckman

The three boys raced back down to the dining room and told Father Jacobi that they found Kenny in a bathroom stall. He wasn't moving. Jacobi hurried out of the dining room to find his assistant,

Father John McHenry. Both Prefects dashed up to the bathroom. Tim Fitzgerald followed them.

Mr. Fitzgerald recalled being so traumatized by Brother Alphonse and what he had seen the previous night that he was afraid to enter the bathroom. He watched from the open door along with Joe Dahlstrom and Harry May, who were already in the bathroom when Fathers Jacobi and McHenry entered.

While Father Jacobi guarded the entrance so no one else could enter or leave, Father McHenry stood in front of the second bathroom stall and called to the boy inside. When there was no response, McHenry pulled on the door, hoping it was not locked. The door did not budge; it did not rattle. McHenry bent down and looked under the door as Pat Beckman had. Then McHenry stood up and ordered a student to fetch a chair which he placed in front of the stall. McHenry peeked over the top.

"This boy is not just sleeping," Father McHenry told Father Jacobi, according to both Dahlstrom and May.

"Out!" Father Jacobi told the boys in the bathroom. "Out!

***

According to a March 10th police report, Fathers Jacobi and McHenry found the boy hanging on the coat hook on the inside of the door. He was dressed in pajamas and had a handkerchief tied around his neck. His feet were "flush with the floor" and he appeared to be dead.

Father McHenry, who was the school football coach and more athletic than Father Jacobi, climbed over the partition, jumped into the stall and opened the door. One priest pushed Kenny's body up while the other slipped the knotted handkerchief off the hook. Then they laid Kenny's body on the floor. Father McHenry rushed out of the bathroom to get a blanket which the two priests spread out on the terrazzo. Then they lifted Kenny's lifeless body, and placed it on the blanket.

Father McHenry guarded the body while Father Jacobi went to report Kenny's death to his superior, Father Charles Malin, the Seminary Rector responsible for the welfare and safety of the staff and the students. Father Malin made his first call to the seminary's attorney, James Voss, who immediately reported Kenneth Rudnitski's death to Walworth County Sheriff's office. According to a March 8, 1960, police report, civilian dispatcher Frank Tooke received Voss's call and recorded it in the log at 7:55 AM, about ten minutes after Fathers Jacobi and McHenry had placed Red's body on the floor. According to the report, Voss told the dispatcher that a "man" at Divine Word Seminary in East Troy Township had committed suicide.

***

Back in his office waiting for the police to arrive, Father Jacobi was apparently so bewildered about why Kenny had hung himself that he called Pat Beckman into his office.

"Do you have any idea what had happened?" Father Jacobi asked Beckman. "Anything bothering Kenny?"

"I don't think so," Beckman said. He had not noticed any strange behavior while pitching pennies with Red the previous day.

Other than the description of the infirmary, the following account is based exclusively on interviews with Mr. Tim Fitzgerald.

***

After Father Jacobi questioned Pat Beckman, Tim Fitzgerald knocked on the prefect's door. He was so confused and in such mental anguish that he went to Father Jacobi for help, even though he didn't completely trust him. Father Jacobi could be kind and solicitous, but just as tough on discipline. It never apparently occurred to Tim to confide in Brother Felix, whom he trusted without reservation.

Although Tim hadn't planned to do so, he told Father Jacobi how Brother Alphonse had assaulted him the previous month in the basement darkroom. He was so emotionally distraught that the words spilled out in a tearful tumble. Father Jacobi seemed uncomfortable with the details of Brother Alphonse's sexual attack but showed no outrage. Nor did he seem surprised. Tim also told Father Jacobi about the two pairs of feet in the stall and that he believed the second pair belonged to Brother Alphonse. Once again Father Jacobi didn't seem surprised.

To make his mental state even more emotionally precarious, the 13-year-old boy felt guilty. If he had reported Brother Alphonse's sexual attack to Father Jacobi, maybe Brother Alphonse's superiors would have transferred him to an institution without boys. Maybe Red would still be alive.

***

Because he could barely stand or walk, Father Jacobi gently picked Tim up and carried him to the lowerclassmen's infirmary, which was tucked in a quiet corner of the seminary, away from the rumble of student voices and the shuffle of feet.

Rev. Paul Jacobi, S.V.D.

The infirmary was a spotless, sterile, rectangular room with eight to ten matching beds lined with precision. Solid-colored blankets covered the beds which were made up military style, ends tucked in and without crease or wrinkle. A chair stood next to each bed. There were no pictures on the white walls. There was no radio, no television.

The dispensary was in another room across the hall. Besides a couple of chairs and a scale, there was a row of hardwood cabinets with shelves containing among other items—aspirin tablets, cough medicine, peroxide, iodine, Band-Aids, and bandages. There was also a logbook that chronicled infirmary and dispensary activity. Mr. Fitzgerald was the only student in the infirmary on the morning of March 8th.

Father Jacobi put Tim to bed and gave him a sedative. The last thing Tim remembered with clarity was Father Jacobi sitting on the chair next to the bed, praying the rosary. Tim spent several days and nights alone in the infirmary, drifting in and out of sleep.

Mr. Fitzgerald's recollections of his time in bed were hazy. Asked what kind of sedative Father Jacobi had given him, he said: "I remember clearly being given some medicine. I have no clue as to what it was. But it wasn't codeine because I mentioned I had an allergy to that."

Asked how long he had spent in the infirmary, Mr. Fitzgerald could not say.

Mid-Morning

The Walworth County Sheriff's Department was typical for a rural Wisconsin county with a population of around 100,000. According to the 1960-61 *Official Directory of Walworth County*, Sheriff Joseph Dorr had between twenty and twenty-five county police officers working for him. Two-thirds were highway patrolmen who cruised rural county roads and byways, investigating vehicular accidents and chasing drunk drivers, speedsters, red-light and stop-sign runners, and unsafe vehicles. Most of the other officers on the Walworth team held desk jobs. That left only three or four full time police detectives to investigate domestic disputes and violence, fist fights, petty thefts, disturbing the peace, nonsupport, and parole violations. Every now and then there would be a major crime such as arson, auto theft, bribery, check kiting, drug possession and trafficking, fraud, robbery, and rape.

On Tuesday, March 8, 1960, Deputy Sheriff Werner Voegeli was the only criminal investigator on call during the eight to three PM shift. Frank Tooke, the dispatcher who recorded the phone call from attorney James Voss, assigned the Rudnitski case to Voegeli.

Tooke's log entry read:

"Claimant: James Voss

Claim: Suicide"

Suicides were not uncommon in Walworth County. According to a U.S. Public Health Service report, there were 10.7 suicide deaths per 100,000 people during the 1960s. According to statistics provided by Walworth County, there were 10 suicides in the county in 1960.

***

With seventeen years of experience as a criminal investigator, Deputy Voegeli, in his mid-forties, was highly trained by 1960 rural county standards. A U.S. Army veteran with the rank of 1st Lieutenant, he worked at Walworth County Lakeland Hospital from 1945 to 1947, when he joined the Walworth County Sheriff's Department at the age of 23. Voegeli did not attend a police academy. His initial investigation training was an apprenticeship under the tutelage of older, experienced detectives.

Deputy Voegeli soon became such a promising and dedicated police investigator that the department sent him to Chicago for polygraph examination certification and then to the U.S. Army's Counter Intelligence Corps' (CIC) academy for advanced criminal investigation training. The school was located on the CIC's sprawling campus at Fort Holabird in Baltimore. The now defunct Maryland academy was to the army what the FBI academy at Quantico, Virginia, was and still is to the Justice Department.

After his CIC training was completed, Deputy Voegeli returned to the Walworth County Sheriff's office as senior investigator and instructor for new recruits. He also set up and was in charge of the police photo laboratory. When Voegeli retired from the police force in 1977 as Chief Deputy Sheriff, the Wisconsin State Legislature passed a citation lauding him for "his many years of outstanding service in police work and the performance of his responsibilities to Walworth County and the State of Wisconsin to protect and defend its citizens."

A freedom of information request for all documents, exhibits, photos, correspondence, memoranda, and reports relating to Walworth County's investigation into the death of Kenneth Rudnitski turned up just three documents—Deputy Voegeli's single-spaced, one and a quarter page investigation report; dispatcher Frank Tooke's one-line entry; and a one-paragraph announcement that the case was closed. *The following description of Walworth County's investigation into the death of Kenneth Rudnitski is based on those three documents and Kenneth Rudnitski's death certificate.*

***

Deputy Sheriff Werner Voegeli lived in William's Bay, Wisconsin, about thirty miles from Divine Word Seminary. He arrived at the school at 9:15 AM, an hour and twenty minutes after attorney James Voss reported Kenny's death to the Sheriff's office in Elkhorn, the county seat. The students were in class.

Father Charles Malin and James Voss were waiting for Deputy Voegeli when he arrived. Missing from the detective's report was what Father Malin and his attorney told him about Kenneth Rudnitski, his death, and the circumstances of his death. Also missing from Voegeli's report was who else was in Father Malin's office that March 8th morning.

Bill Burrows and his work-partner George Engemann visited Father Malin's office during March 8th morning recess. Bill and George were installing an intercom from the projection booth to the back stage of the auditorium for communication during plays and other events. Father Malin had complained to the Prefect Father Jacobi that the boys used a substantial amount of phone wire without permission. Father Jacobi sent Burrows and Engemann to Father Malin's office to explain how they got the wire.

George Engemann

Mr. Engemann is a U.S. Air Force Vietnam War veteran. He was ill and could not be interviewed. Mr. Burrows was eventually ordained, earned a PhD in Christian Theology from the University of Chicago Divinity School, and became an editor, historical researcher, and prolific writer. He is recognized as an expert on world religions and history of the Catholic Church. As Mr. Burrows recalled:

He and Engemann opened the outer door to Father Malin's office, walked down a narrow ten-foot inner hallway, and knocked on Father Malin's inner door. When Father Malin opened it, Burrows glanced inside before Father Malin shut it.

"I saw a uniformed [police] officer and several people sitting in the office," Mr. Burrows recalled. "I don't remember the number." Burrows went on to say he didn't remember seeing Father Jacobi and/or his assistant Father McHenry in the room. Other than the police officer, the men he saw were wearing business suits.

Father Malin ushered the two boys out of the inner hallway into the main corridor, then closed the outer door behind him. Burrows and Engemann explained to Father Malin that they did not take the wire without permission. Brother Albert, who was in charge of the supply room, had given it to them. Father Malin listened to the explanation without interrupting. Mr. Burrows recalled him saying: "Okay. I'm sorry for the misunderstanding."

The only outsiders at the school that morning were attorney James Voss, Deputy Sheriff Werner Voegeli, County Consulting Physician Dr. Ross Baker, and County Coroner Osmund Bakkom.

***

After his meeting with Father Malin and Voss, Deputy Voegeli viewed Kenneth Rudnitski's body, which was still stretched out on a blanket on the bathroom floor. Voegeli noted that Kenny was barefoot and dressed in pajamas. There was a handkerchief tightly wrapped around his neck. Voegeli examined the handkerchief and noted that the ends were tied in a common granny knot and that the handkerchief had the name "Rudnitski" sewn on the edge. (Kenny sent his clothes to a laundry in East Troy which required the students to have either their name or a laundry number on each piece of clothing.) Deputy Voegeli emphasized in his report that, from what he could see of Red's clothed body, there were no signs of a struggle or foul play.

After his visual inspection of the body, Detective Voegeli entered the bathroom stall. He saw a pair of slippers resting side by side on the terrazzo floor. They pointed to the rear wall, twelve inches in front of and six inches to the right of the toilet. Voegeli also saw an aspirin tablet on the floor near the slippers. He noted that the coat hook on the stall door was bent downward as far as it could go and that the door lock was jammed with toilet paper.

Once again, Voegeli emphasized in his brief report that he found "no evidence of a struggle or foul play" inside the stall, which complemented his observations on the corpse. If Deputy Voegeli took photos, they were not provided under a freedom of information request.

Mid-Morning

The Walworth County Sheriff's office assigned Dr. Ross Baker to perform the preliminary examination of Kenneth Rudnitski's body. It was common practice in 1960 for a practicing physician to conduct the preliminary examination of a corpse and provide a death certificate. It was also common practice for the examining physician to conduct his own autopsy, if deemed necessary or advisable.

Like Deputy Werner Voegeli, Baker was highly trained and experienced. According to his April 1984 obituary in the *Elkhorn Independent*, Baker was born in Ontario, Canada, and received the degree of Doctor of Osteopathy (DO) from the Chicago College of Osteopathy and Surgery in 1941. Baker was not a trained medical examiner. It was not unusual in 1960 to assign a family practitioner to review a corpse, according to consulting forensic pathologist Dr. Joseph Hodge.

Like Officer Voegeli, Dr. Baker served in the military during World War II—as a Medical Officer in the Royal Canadian Air Force. Like Voegeli, Dr. Baker settled in East Troy in 1947 where he opened a family clinic as a family doctor and surgeon with a specialty in "General Practice" (credential #10878-21).

Dr. Baker was a member of both the American and the Wisconsin Osteopathic Association and the American College of General Practitioners. When he retired in 1981, after tending to the medical needs of the East Troy Township for thirty-four years, the Greater East Troy Chamber of Commerce honored Dr. Baker for "his dedication and service to the community.

Dr. Baker's official duty as a Walworth County consulting physician was to perform a *preliminary examination* of Kenneth Rudnitski's body and pronounce the boy dead. According to the 1960 Wisconsin death certificate form, Dr. Baker was expected to record an estimated time of death, and the cause, manner, mode of death. The form also wanted to know how long it took the subject to die. If Dr. Baker could not determine a cause of death or found the death to be suspicious, it was his duty to recommend an autopsy to the County Coroner, according to Wisconsin law.

A request to the Walworth County Medical Examiner's Office for any and all documents, photos, and notes dealing with Dr. Baker and/or Kenneth Rudnitski turned up nothing. If Dr. Baker took any notes during his brief examination of Red's corpse, they have been lost or destroyed. *The following outline of a preliminary inspection of a corpse in 1960 is therefore based on descriptions provided by medical professionals.*

***

Under normal room temperature, a dead body begins to lose heat at the approximate rate of 1-1.5 degrees per hour. To estimate the approximate time of death, a medical doctor checked Kenny's body for rigor mortis. A corpse begins to stiffen and contract approximately fifteen minutes after death occurs, depending on the temperature of the room and the location of the body. A corpse found in a room with a normal nighttime temperature would attain full rigor at around fifteen hours. It would disappear in approximately thirty-six hours.

To determine the state of rigor mortis, the examining doctor probed Kenny's body with his fingers for the degree and the depth of rigor stiffness. The condition of the eyes offered another time-of-death clue. Soon after death occurs, the optic fluid in the eyes begins to dry. Irises change shape. The pupils dilate and progressively fail to react to light.

The medical doctor checked the corpse for knife or gunshot wounds, broken bones, bruises, suspicious marks, and signs of sexual assault. The doctor examined the eyes to determine if the subject died of asphyxiation which causes petechiae—capillary ruptures manifested as pin-point red dots.

***

After completing the preliminary examination and declaring Kenneth Rudnitski dead, Dr. Baker told Detective Voegeli—according to the Deputy Sheriff's report—that Kenneth Rudnitski died "about 12m" (midnight). Like Deputy Voegeli, Baker found "no signs of foul play or struggle" and concluded that Kenneth Rudnitski died from asphyxiation by hanging and that his death was a suicide. Dr. Baker expressed no doubts about his findings and did not request an autopsy for confirmation.

Walworth County Coroner Osmund L. Bakkom was present during Dr. Baker's examination of Kenny's body on Tuesday morning, March 8. Mr. Bakkom was an elected official and a real estate broker. Wisconsin's 1960 statutes did not require a county coroner to have either a medical degree or any specialized medical training. It wasn't his job to determine cause of death. As agent of the County and the State, Bakkom (credential #36347-90) was only an administrator and a facilitator.

In the case of Kenneth Rudnitski, Bakkom's main job was to make sure that Dr. Baker determined the cause of death. If Baker could not do so, had doubts about the cause of death, or found the death "suspicious," Coroner Bakkom would order an autopsy and officially record the cause of death as determined by the person who performed the autopsy. Wisconsin did not mandate autopsies for suicides in 1960.

Coroner Bakkom accepted Dr. Baker's finding of suicide and saw no need to order an autopsy. Kenny's parents, Gladys and Joseph Rudnitski, had the right to request one under Wisconsin State Law. They chose not to. Bakkom released Kenny's body to Helzer Funeral Home in East Troy.

Late Morning

After completing his visual inspection of the bathroom stall and getting a verbal confirmation of death by suicide from Dr. Baker, Deputy Voegeli interviewed Fathers Paul Jacobi, John McHenry, and Charles Malin. What was missing in Voegeli's investigation was a *motive* for why a 15-year-old boy would hang himself with his own handkerchief in a bathroom around midnight. As a result, the questions Voegeli asked the three priests were all directed at motive.

The following account is based entirely on Detective Voegeli's report.

***

Fathers Jacobi and McHenry characterized Kenneth Rudnitski as:
"A poor student
Had a difficult time in making his grades
Poorly talented
Very nervous
Easily upset
About third from the bottom of his class"
Detective Voegeli went on to report: "The fathers have had numerous conferences with the boy. However, not recently. No sickness or despondency noted of late. Boy last seen alive at bedtime by other boys. Nothing wrong noted."
During interviews with Detective Voegeli, Father Jacobi said that he first heard of the bare feet in bathroom stall number two from Ray Miles, a freshman, not from Pat Beckman. And Father McHenry volunteered that he had gotten up between midnight and one AM to use the student bathroom. His bedroom, which was near the student lavatory, had a shaving sink but no toilet.

```
7272                    3/8/60                              Voegeli

TYPE OF COMPLAINT:          SUICIDE

COMPLAINANT:            James Voss

COMPLAINANT'S ADDRESS:          E. Troy ID

Call received from above at 7:55am date ref help needed at the Devine Lord
Seminary just out of East Troy - same reported a man found dead in the bldg.

Arrived Seminary about 8:15am - contacted Voss and Father Charles Maling
also Fathers Paul Jacobi and John Cheney; was advised as follows:
RUDNITZKI, Kenneth Robert 15 (4/16/44) of 1614 Barham Ave., Janesville, Wisc.
has been a student since September 1958 - in his second year at the seminary.
Deceased was a poor student, had a difficult time in making his grades,
poorly talented, very nervous and easily upset and shook.  Was about third
from the bottom of his class of about thirty boys.  The Fathers have had
numerous conferences with the boy, however not recently.  No sickness or
despondency noted of late.  Boy was last seen alive at bedtime by the other
boys, nothing wrong noted.  About 12m to last date Father McHenry went to
the washroom (located on the third floor, next to his own room) and went
into the first toilet booth - at that time he noted a pair of slippers on
the floor of the booth next to his and also saw the feet of a boy facing
the toilet bowl but no words were exchanged and he returned to his room.

The boys got up at 6am as usual and the same as always made a dash for the
washroom and several boys noted the deceased in the second booth but didn't
think anything about it.  Raymond Miles a student reported to Father Jacobi
at about 7:40am date that he had returned to the washroom and found the
deceased was still there and thought it strange.  Fathers Jacobi and McHenry
went to the washroom, called to RUDNITZKI and after no answer looked over
the top of the partition and discovered the deceased hanging by a handkerchief
on the clothes hook on the back of the door - the door lock was jammed with
some toilet paper.  The one Father cut the boy down while the other held him;
stated that his feet were flush with the floor - then laid him on a blanket
in front of the door, and called E. Troy ID.

The handkerchief used by the boy had his last name sewn into the edge as is
customery, same had been tied with a granny knot at opposite corners.
Weight of the body bent the upper hook down onto the lower up curved part.
No evidence of any struggle or foul play.

Dr. Baker of E. Troy came to scene and pronounced the boy dead; no question
in his mind - estimated the time of death at about 12m.  Coroner Bakkom to
scene for the information, also satisfied and called it a suicide.

Parents; Joseph and Gladys Rudnitzki will be notified by Father Jacobi in
person am date.

Body taken to Helser Funeral Home, E. Troy.
```

Father McHenry told Detective Voegeli that he noticed the bare feet in the second stall. After he entered the first stall, McHenry said, he locked the door, bent down, and peeked under the partition. McHenry confirmed that the feet he saw were firmly planted on the floor and were pointing toward the toilet bowl. The priest also told Voegeli that he saw a pair of slippers next to the toilet.

Rev. John McHenry, S.V.D.

"No words were exchanged before Father McHenry returned to his room," Deputy Voegeli reported.

Deputy Sheriff Werner Voegeli did not interview any priests besides Fathers Malin, Jacobi, and McHenry. Nor did he interview any brothers or students. He signed his report without reaching a conclusion and without commenting on the cause, manner, and mode of death. He left those determinations entirely up to Dr. Ross Baker and the confirmation of Baker's conclusion up to Coroner Osmund Bakkom. Deputy Voegeli did not report that the death of Kenneth Rudnitski looked suspicious in any way.

Having completed a one-hour investigation, Deputy Werner Voegeli drove back to the sheriff's office in Elkhorn to write a 1¼-page report.

Mid-Afternoon

After Deputy Sheriff Werner Voegeli left the seminary and returned to his office in Elkhorn, Father Charles Malin faced an urgent problem. Red's hometown paper, the *Janesville Daily Gazette* (circulation around 14,000) published an article titled "Janesville Seminarian Hangs Self," in its afternoon edition, just seven hours after Fathers Jacobi and McHenry laid Red's body on the bathroom floor. Janesville was the Rock County Seat, the county's largest city, the tenth largest city in Wisconsin, and one of the most influential newspapers in southern Wisconsin. The un-bylined article stated:

"The Sheriff's office department this morning investigated the death of a Janesville student at Divine Word Seminary near East Troy. The body of Kenneth R. Rudnitski, 15, of 1614 Barnham Avenue, was discovered suspended by a knotted handkerchief from the coat hook in a locked cubicle of the washroom. Coroner Osmund Bakkom ruled the death a suicide."

There was a risk that the Milwaukee newspapers would pick up on the *Gazette* story and cause widespread public relations damage. There could be an in-depth follow-up story by a suspicious investigative reporter which might provoke a formal criminal investigation mounted by the county prosecutor.

The biggest threat came from the evening *Milwaukee Journal* and the morning *Milwaukee Sentinel*. Both papers enjoyed state-wide circulation and the *Journal* had an excellent national reputation.

Father Malin sought help from Moses E. Kiley, Archbishop of the Diocese of Milwaukee, which included East Troy. Very soon after the discovery of Red's body on Tuesday, March 8, either Father Malin or his attorney James Voss contacted the Archdiocese to "intervene" with the *Journal* and the *Sentinel* to keep the suicide story out of their papers.

***

In response to a request for all records dealing with Divine Word Seminary (especially reports on Brother Alphonse Horne) Shelly

Taylor, Director of Archives and Records Management for the Archdiocese of Milwaukee, responded in a letter saying: "The Archdiocese does not have records of Divine Word Seminary [which] was under the jurisdiction of the religious order, not the Archdiocese." Religious orders are autonomous in dealing with internal matters.

Taylor went on to say that she/he found a relevant letter in the folder containing correspondence between Divine Word Seminary and the Chancery. "While not much," Taylor wrote, "I hope it is helpful to your research."

Dated Sunday March 13, 1960, five days after Red's death, the short letter was written by Father Malin to Monsignor Leo L. Brust. As Chancellor of the Archdiocese, Brust was chief record keeper and archivist for the archdiocese, top trouble shooter, legal notary, and manager of chancery offices and personnel. Msgr. Brust would be appointed Bishop Brust the following year, 1961, and serve as a diocesan Auxiliary Bishop.

Malin's letter to Brust in its entirety read:

Rt. Reverend and dear Monsignor Brust: Just a note to thank you for your wonderful kindness toward us during these dark days for our little seminary. Your intervention in our behalf with the Milwaukee Journal and the Sentinel has done much to save our good name.

We buried the young man Friday. Five of us Fathers were there and the two nights of the wake we also had some Fathers present. Since the family is hard pressed for means I also requested to be allowed to help and sent them three hundred dollars. It was a hard blow to all of us, and your timely help will not be forgotten.

Thanking you again, I remain,
Yours in our Blessed Mother,
(Rev.) Charles M. Malin

A review of the available archives of the *Milwaukee Journal* and *Sentinel* failed to find any articles on the death of Kenneth Rudnitski or any mention of him in passing.

***

Without exception, the former students who were interviewed said they were shocked and confused when they heard rumors on Tuesday March 8th that Kenny was dead. The lowerclassmen, who were the closest to Red, were especially dazed. Pat Beckman, Jerome Richter, and Larry Shaddig were talking about finding Red hanging in a bathroom stall. So were Joe Dahlstrom and Harry May, who were in the bathroom when Father McHenry stood on a chair, peeked over the top of the door and pronounced: "This boy isn't just sleeping."

The former students noted during their interviews that Red seemed happy the previous day, Monday March 7th. Mr. Beckman recalled pitching pennies with Red on the sidewalk in front of the building. He was his usual cheerful and competitive self, Mr. Beckman said.

Mr. Dahlstrom recalled joking with Red during supper about how much food he wolfed down. He ate like it was "his last supper," Dahlstrom said.

Mr. Hahner recalled shooting baskets with Red in the gym. "If there were mood swings, he didn't express them," Hahner said.

Mr. Kairis recalled Red having fun in the rec room that night. "Red was goofing around as if he had no care in the world. Happy as a lark," Kairis said.

And Deputy Sheriff Voegeli reported that none of the students noted anything unusual about Red in the dormitory before lights-out at 8:45.

Late-Afternoon

It was Father Paul Jacobi's task as Head Prefect to confirm what many, but not all, students already knew—Kenny Rudnitski was dead. What they didn't know were the details of the how and the why.

Around 5:00 PM on Tuesday March 8th, nine hours after he laid Kenny's body on the bathroom floor, Father Jacobi addressed the students. Most of Red's classmates and fellow students either couldn't recall where the address took place after sixty years or thought it may have been in the chapel. Mike Walsh, a freshman in 1960, recalled with clarity that the address took place in the study hall. If there was no consensus on where Father Jacobi delivered his message, there was unanimity about what he said in a tone that was nervous and somber:

Father Jacobi announced that Kenny was dead. He was so troubled he took his own life. But he was not responsible. All we can do now is pray for him and for his family. Father Jacobi went on to order the students not to discuss Kenny's death among themselves. It was best to pray and forget and to let Kenny rest in peace. Father Jacobi also warned the students not to write home about Kenny's death. The faculty would be sending a letter to their parents explaining what had happened. If any student wrote anything about Kenny in a letter, Father Jacobi warned, the letter would not be posted. He did not use the word "suicide" in his address, nor did he offer a group prayer. He did not welcome questions.

Dick Hahner, among other students, found no warmth or comfort in Father Jacobi's comments, no help coping with his grief.

Richard Hahner

After Jacobi's address, which the former students described as shocking, confusing, and incomplete, word began to spread through the school—in spite of the order not to talk about Kenny—that Brother Alphonse had something to do with Red's death. None of the former students who were interviewed liked Brother Alphonse. Most said they avoided him as best they could because he was "creepy" and so unlike Brothers Felix and Jude. The students who had been approached by Brother Alphonse or who had been inappropriately touched by him lent oxygen to those suspicions. So did the fact that Brother Alphonse had vanished.

"No one saw him," Mr. Dahlstrom recalled. "No one found him."

Joe Dahlstrom

Brother Alphonse wasn't cleaning floors or hanging around the locker room and shower room, the former students reported. Rather than calm their fears, his absence intensified them. Why was Alphonse hiding if he didn't do something bad to Red?

By bedtime on March 8th, most of the former students reported being scared. What if Brother Alphonse crept into the dormitory while they were sleeping? What if he sexually attacked someone, smothered someone with a pillow, strangled someone? Their fear was so real that some boys made pacts with a friend—if one had to go to the bathroom during the night, the other would go along with him. Some huddled together.

"I was terribly frightened to go back into the dormitory," Mr. Hahner recalled. "My bed was close to the lavatory. We were all on edge. I remember pulling my bed frame close to Harry May's. We had a baseball bat for protection. I slept with it."

Thursday March 10th

Mid-Morning

On Thursday morning March 10th, two days after Father Jacobi told the students that Kenny Rudnitski had sadly taken his own life, Joe Dahlstrom was sick in bed in the dormitory. Dahlstrom was one of the students who had witnessed Father McHenry climb on a chair in the bathroom and look over the top of the stall where he saw Kenny's blue bare feet.

Popular with his classmates, Joe Dahlstrom was a varsity football player along with Ed Harte who caught Alphonse abusing Red in the dormitory on the night he died, and with Pat Beckman who found Red's body hanging in the bathroom stall.

Like Dick Hahner, Ed Harte, and Tim Fitzgerald, Mr. Dahlstrom was a Vietnam War veteran. Like Dick Hahner, he graduated from Officer Candidate School with the rank of 2nd Lieutenant. The 1960 year book described Joe Dahlstrom as: "Huge. This applied not only to his corporal appearance, but to his fun-loving disposition. [He] holds fast to that old fashioned 'Show Me' attitude."

Mr. Dahlstrom could not remember why he took sick on that March 10th morning sixty years ago. But he clearly remembered that Father Jacobi sent him to the dormitory instead of to the infirmary, which was the logical place for a sick student. The infirmary was a quiet haven where Father Jacobi could tend to him until he was well enough to return to class. Furthermore, if Dahlstrom was suffering from something contagious, a bed in the infirmary would protect the other students.

Asked "Why the dormitory?" Mr. Dahlstrom said: "Probably because the infirmary was full." Tim Fitzgerald recalled being the only student in the infirmary at the time.

While Dahlstrom was resting in bed, he heard voices coming from the front of the building that overlooked Lake Beulah, still imprisoned under a layer of dull gray ice. What Dahlstrom heard that morning sounded like an angry argument, loud but not screaming.

Dahlstrom hopped out of bed and rushed to a window. He saw Brother Felix dressed in his black cassock "walking" a reluctant Brother Alphonse down the front steps. Brother Alphonse was dressed in civilian clothes. He had an overcoat slung over his arm. Brother Felix "walked" him to a car parked in front of the school. Then he pushed Brother Alphonse inside and drove off. Word quickly spread throughout the seminary that Brother Alphonse was gone.

"We all began to relax," Mr. May recalled.

Also on Thursday, March 10, 1960, two days after the death of Kenny Rudnitski, Dr. Ross Baker signed the boy's death certificate which read:

> Cause of Death: Asphyxiation—strangulation.
>
> Due to: Hanging.
>
> Death occurred: Approximately midnight.
>
> Describe how injury occurred: By hanging himself on back (illegible) bathroom door.
>
> Accident/Suicide/Homicide: Dr. Baker indicated "suicide."
>
> Interval Between Onset and Death: 2

The "2" meant that, according to Dr. Baker, it took Rudnitski two hours to die of asphyxiation.

WISCONSIN STATE BOARD OF HEALTH
ORIGINAL CERTIFICATE OF DEATH

Also on March 10, 1960, two days after Kenny's death and after Dr. Ross Baker signed Kenny's death certificate, someone at the Walworth County Sheriff's Office wrote in longhand on form No. 7072:

"Kenneth Rudzinski
DOB 4-10-44
Died 3-8-60 by hanging
At Divine Word Seminary"

The initials of the reporter were illegible and Kenneth's last name was misspelled. An entry on the form read:

CASE CLOSED

Friday March 11th

Morning

At eight o'clock in the morning on Friday, March 11th, twenty-seven of Red's classmates piled into the old red and white converted Greyhound bus that the school mainly used to ferry the football and basketball teams to outside games. Father Paul Jacobi sat behind the wheel. The boys were on their way to St. William's Church in Janesville, thirty miles away, to attend Red's funeral. It was three days after Red's dead body was found hanging in the bathroom stall. It was one day after the Walworth County Sheriff closed the Rudnitski case as a suicide. The students were not given the option to stay home.

Several seminary priests attended the wake the previous night and five seminary priests attended the funeral itself, according to Father Malin's letter to Msgr. Leo Brust. Four of Red's classmates served the funeral mass, three were pallbearers.

***

The students sat side by side, their heads bowed in grief during the bus ride to St. William's Church. A profound sadness hung over the bus. It was so quiet during the one-hour ride to Janesville that, as Mr. Bud May put it: "You could hear a pin drop." Once inside St. William's Church, the students filed into the pews reserved for them. Most of Red's classmates were still struggling with Father Jacobi's announcement that Red had taken his own life.

"We were still in shock," Mr. Kairis recalled. "There was disbelief it happened. How the hell could this happen?"

Surrounded by stained glass windows and the calming scent of incense, Red's classmates realized that they could no longer deny that their friend was really dead. For some like Bob Kairis, the funeral settled their nagging doubt about Red committing suicide. "I was confused," Mr. Kairis recalled. "But I finally accepted it."

Robert Kairis

The only thing about the funeral service that Red's classmates remembered clearly was the sobbing of Red's parents, Joseph and Gladys; his eight brothers, James, David, Richard, Alan, Norman, Robert, Stephen and Joseph; and his three sisters, Joann, Mary, and Ann Theresa. The family sat in the front pew, close to Red's coffin which was draped in black and had a brass crucifix staring back at them. Kenny's 16th birthday would have been the next month on April 10th.

Family tears became infectious. "The funeral was so sad," Mr. Dahlstrom recalled. "I was overwhelmed. The students were crying."

After the Church service, the boys silently ate lunch in the church hall. Then they boarded the bus for home. On the way to the funeral, sadness hovered over the bus. On the way back, there was more sorrow than sadness. No one talked about the funeral or how they felt; Father Jacobi's directive of silence was still in force and would be until school adjourned in June. Father Jacobi was driving the bus.

***

It is difficult to paint a detailed description of Red's funeral or to be more specific in reporting the full impact the event had on his classmates:

According to the funeral report recorded by Snyder's Funeral Home, the three seminary pallbearers were Red's friends: Pat Beckman, Jerome Richter, and Bruce La Montaigne. Beckman and Richter could not remember being pallbearers. La Montaigne thought he might have been one but could not be sure.

Not a single former student could recall who served the mass, not even the altar boys themselves.

No one could remember which seminary priests attended the funeral other than Father Jacobi who drove the bus.

No one could remember the slow procession out of St. William's Church with the Rudnitski family trailing behind the coffin.

No one could remember the singing of the traditional Gregorian chant hymn: *In Paradisum Deducant Te Angeli* ("May the Angels Lead You into Paradise").

"I've tried hard to remember," Mr. May said, "But I just don't have any memories." He suggested that he may have repressed them.

Mr. Laka, who had a good memory on other issues, couldn't even remember going to the funeral.

Greg Laka

Saturday March 12th

Evening

By Saturday, March 12th, the day after Red's funeral and four days after his death, whispers about Brother Alphonse were still "running all over the place," Mr. Koleno recalled. The fact that Brother Felix had driven Brother Alphonse away and that no one had seen him since only confirmed the suspicion that Alphonse had something to do with Red's death. Father Charles Malin addressed those whispers.

***

Somewhat rotund and soon to earn the nickname "Chunky Charlie," Father Malin had spent most of his twenty-three years after ordination as a high school Seminary Prefect. As Rector, he wore many hats. He was the religious superior of the Fathers and Brothers at the Seminary. He was the Principal of the school. He was tasked with keeping the school financially sound, enforcing the rules, and solving problems.

As a person, Father Charles Malin was a complex man, an "enigma," according to a former priest who knew him well. After his ordination in 1937, Father Malin spent his first year as a Procurator (financial manager) at the East Troy seminary. Years later, he brought a Procurator's mentality into his Rector's office, where he was known as a paperclip counter who frequently dressed students down for wasting supplies during their work assignments or for using supplies without his explicit permission. Father Malin's attention to detail compelled him to litter his office floor with scraps of paper and notes to himself. More important, he was known by his fellow priests as a loner who kept mostly to himself and avoided parties and get-togethers.

As a priest, however, Father Malin was kind, caring, and gentle, according to former students who had personal dealings with him. Even though he was concerned about balancing the seminary books, he would admit students from struggling families tuition-free or forgive the monthly payments they could not honor. That made Father Malin, as Mr. May put it, "a strong person who wore a friendly face."

Father Malin chose to deliver his message to the students in the chapel on Saturday March 12th, five days after Red's death. Every Saturday evening, the students gathered for "Compline," an ancient monastic night prayer. The East Troy adaptation consisted of reciting psalms, singing Gregorian chants, and listening to a sermon delivered by the Rector. It was an end-of-the-week moment to call on God to bless the seminary, guide its priests and brothers, and keep the students safe. At the end of Compline Father Malin offered Benediction of the Blessed Sacrament in an ornate cope (cape) and the chapel was blessed with sacred incense. *The following account of Malin's remarks to the students is based on thirteen interviews with former seminary students who were present in the chapel on Saturday, March 12th, 1960.*

***

For his sermon that March 12th Saturday night, Father Malin was dressed in a black cassock, white surplice, and a purple stole. It was Lent, the liturgical season before Easter, and purple was its liturgical color.

Like Father Jacobi, who had issued his mandate of silence five days earlier, Father Malin got right to the point. As he stood in the sanctuary with candles flickering on the altar behind him, Father Malin told the students that he had been informed of certain rumors about a certain staff member. The students who are spreading those false rumors are destroying that staff member's reputation. That is calumny. And calumny is a mortal sin. For the sake of your immortal soul, stop spreading those rumors. Stop listening to those rumors.

Father Malin never mentioned Brother Alphonse by name.

"I felt like he was talking straight to me," Mr. Fitzgerald recalled. "I'm going straight to hell for telling Father Jacobi about Brother Alphonse."

Very Rev. Charles Malin, S.V.D.

Father Charles Malin was not just protecting Brother Alphonse, the seminary, his religious order, and the Church. He was protecting himself as well. Like Brother Alphonse, Father Charles Malin was a sexual predator.

The following account is based on interviews with Mr. Timothy Fitzgerald.

Father Malin knew that Tim was fatherless, vulnerable, and a ward of the state of Illinois at Angel Guardian Orphanage. During Tim's freshman year, Father Malin had always been warm and caring to his impoverished mother, and as far as 13-year-old Tim Fitzgerald was concerned: "Father Malin could walk on water."

Things changed during Tim's sophomore year. Father Malin began seeking him out during work periods when he was alone. Malin liked to caress Tim's cheek. "You don't even shave yet," Malin said one day after a caress.

One day, Father Malin invited Tim into his office. Then he invited Tim into his bedroom. Father Malin did not physically assault Tim during the bedroom visit. He just unzipped his own pants in front of Tim and masturbated into a towel. And so it was that Tim Fitzgerald became one of "Malin's boys."

***

In June 1961, the year after Red's death, Father Malin told Tim Fitzgerald that he would be attending a meeting of high school seminary librarians at another Divine Word Seminary in Bordentown, New Jersey. Malin was expanding and up-grading the East Troy library. Bill Burrows and his work partner, George Engemann, were installing new bookshelves. Fitzgerald was helping Father Malin with clerical work.

"Would you like to go?" Malin asked Tim.

"You'll have to get permission from the orphanage," Fitzgerald said.

Tim returned to Angel Guardian Orphanage in Chicago for the summer, while the other students went home to their families. One day, with the permission of orphanage director Msgr. Leo Diebold, Father Malin picked Tim up and took him as his traveling companion to the Bordentown meeting. Soon after they arrived by car, Father Jacobi spotted Tim.

"What are *you* doing here?" Father Jacobi asked.

"Father Malin asked me to come with him," Tim said.

Father Jacobi's face changed from surprise to shock, Mr. Fitzgerald recalled. It took a few seconds for him to digest what he had just heard. Father Jacobi did not say a word. Mr. Fitzgerald said that he got the distinct impression that Father Jacobi either knew or suspected that Father Malin was a sexual predator.

Father Jacobi ordered Tim to leave with two brothers who were returning to the Midwest. They dropped him off at Angel Guardian.

Mid-March 1960

In the weeks following the tragic death of Red Rudnitski, Divine Word Seminary became a deeply troubled school. The morale was so low that Father Jacobi called four student leaders into his office. One, Marty Koleno, "felt honored" to be singled out by Father Jacobi. The 1960 school yearbook described Koleno as:

"Another of our music-minded juniors who directs all his attention to the band. Marty played both varsity basketball and football. When he's not participating in sports, he is usually shooting his camera at some unsuspecting prey."

Martin Koleno

"How can we make this go away?" Father Jacobi asked Koleno.

When none of the boys could come up with a solution, Father Jacobi appointed them as a "special committee to raise the spirit of the school," Mr. Koleno recalled. The committee returned to Father Jacobi with two popular suggestions. Even though it was Lent, the students should be allowed to go on a store-hike, which meant they were free to buy their favorite junk foods. And although it was Lent, the students should be treated to a movie. Father Jacobi agreed to both suggestions. The movie was "The Big Circus."

Fresh air, junk food, and a seat at the "Circus" offered only momentary relief; they did not solve a problem that ran much deeper than low morale.

"Divine Word Seminary was a morose, tight-lipped, confusing place," Mr. Hahner recalled. "There was tension from the Prefects and Father Malin. Brother Jude was not laughing as much. The place was never the same."

"Even the faculty seemed upset and depressed," Mr. Koleno recalled.

There is no doubt that the tragic death of Red Rudnitski was traumatic for the students, especially the lowerclassmen, at Divine Word Seminary. In their own words:

"No one could sleep." (Mr. Laka)

"I had a lot of nightmares. I have been haunted all these years." (Mr. Beckman)

"It was spooky. We were covered by a blanket of fear." (Mr. Dahlstrom)

"I was shocked. The night before his death, Red was as happy as a lark. Even today, I still feel shock. Even today." (Mr. Kairis)

"I felt the loss of a friend. Sorry and upset...My final memory of Red was pitching pennies. I hold that memory dear." (Mr. Richter)

"I bought the suicide, but I found it hard to believe. I felt sick and angry...My God, his family is living with this tragedy!" (Mr. LaMontaigne)

"Disbelief. How could this happen?...When I heard Brother Alphonse was involved, it made me suspicious." (Mr. Stommes)

"I believed what [Father Jacobi] said, but I could not see Red hanging himself. It affected me deeply. [So did] not talking to Mom and Dad...I could have done more. I felt guilty about violating the rule not to talk about it...My heart went out to the lowerclassmen who were all afraid of Alphonse." (Mr. Koleno)

"I never bought the suicide story. I was feeling confused, in shock. I was numb for a week. I didn't want to do much of anything. I could not remember anything in Red's demeanor or actions that made me think he could have committed suicide. I'm not a psychologist, but I'm sure as hell not stupid. Suicide made no sense...Our fear was a somewhat undefined fear of Alphonse and the unknown...I think there was some suppression of emotion...I heard someone say: 'Let Alphonse do his job but stay away from him. He's one brother not to be alone with'...There was only one suspect. Alphonse must have had something to do with Red's death. No one else could have done it." (Mr. May)

Bud May

"I felt guilt. I talked about Kenny and Alphonse when I was ordered not to. I felt panic. I couldn't handle the abuse, what I saw, and the guilt. I felt Father Jacobi never took me seriously. I felt stigmatized. My anxiety was palpable. I never felt safe again. The seminary itself was a threat." (Mr. Fitzgerald)

"I was confused. I was scared but didn't know exactly why until talk turned to Alphonse. By the time we went to evening chapel, I was just as confused but now I was scared. I thought Alphonse did something bad to Rudnitski. I may have cried that night after lights out. I have never felt so alone. I had a fear of the dark, being alone in the large seminary building, not wanting to get up alone at night. I was scared every time I had to be in the basement level—corridor, shower room, lavatories. I hated to clean those areas alone...I was wishing I were home, not knowing what to write to my parents. Not allowed to talk about it with each other. Ordered, under the pain of mortal sin, not to imagine, speculate, or listen to rumors. Only to pray for Kenneth...But I was not angry. Priests would never lie to us." (Mr. Hahner)

2020-2021

The interviews with Red's classmates and fellow students also revealed the scope and depth of a life-long pain. They described their doubts that Red had committed suicide, their scars, and their open wounds. They said that the conversation always seemed to turn to Red's death when they got together for the annual alumni retreat at the site of the old seminary.

For years after Red's death, Greg Laka, a Chicago area businessman, said a silent prayer on March 8th, the anniversary of Red's death...Bob Kairis, a steel mill supervisor, still feels the shock of Red's death. He never talks about it. He doesn't know why...Jerome Richter, a software consultant, treasures his last memory of his friend Red pitching pennies on the sidewalk the day before he died. He still sees Red's body hanging on the door hook in bathroom stall number two.

Some of Red's former classmates and fellow students still accept Father Jacobi's announcement that Kenny Rudnitski took his own life. But they were confused in 1960 and are still troubled because they have no answer to "why." Others like Bud May, a quality control engineer and computer science teacher, did not believe Red committed suicide in 1960 and he has not changed his mind. He is still troubled by the question: "If Red didn't commit suicide what happened to him?" It never made sense to Harry May 1960. It still doesn't make sense to Bud May today. And Pat Beckman, a farm owner and manager, has suffered nightmares. He still sees Red's body hanging on the clothes hook in the bathroom stall. "I was haunted all these years," he said.

No one was more affected by the tragic death of Red than Ed Harte, Tim Fitzgerald, and Dick Hahner.

***

Ed Harte enlisted in the Marines and became a boot camp platoon leader. After basic training, the Marines offered him Officer

Candidate School (OSC). He turned it down. Mr. Harte blames Divine Word Seminary for that hasty decision "to just be one of the troops." It was a decision Mr. Harte regrets to this day.

"I looked for leadership and direction from Fathers Jacobi and McHenry," Mr. Harte recalled. "I didn't find any. My experience at East Troy left an indelible mark on me and considerable anger and distrust for superiors in general. I lost my vocation to the priesthood. I lost my faith. I carried that negativity for many years. May those who prey on our youth and those who turn their heads be damned in hell."

Instead of Officer Candidate School, the Corps sent Harte to Sea School to prepare him for service on a ship. After graduation, he was deployed to the Attack Aircraft Carrier *USS Ranger* during the Vietnam War.

Mr. Harte had been warned that he would be receiving a phone call from a writer working on a book about Red. He was ready. He sounded as if he had been waiting sixty years for the chance to tell someone how he saw Brother Alphonse assaulting his friend Kenny "Red" Rudnitski, on the night he died. He wept and blamed himself, a 16-year old boy, for not stopping Brother Alphonse that night, for freezing in shock.

"Why? Why? Why?" Mr. Harte kept repeating during the interview. "I have carried this all my life. I've had flashbacks. I picture Red on his bed not far from me, his head bent down. I see Alphonse staring at me. I've felt sinful. I struggled with my faith. I carry guilt. Why didn't I do something?"

After the two-hour interview, Ed Harte sought out a priest, went to confession, and attended Sunday mass.

***

Tim Fitzgerald enlisted in the U.S. army at the age of nineteen. He served in the 23 Special Warfare Aviation Detachment in Vietnam. He went on search and destroy missions as a member of a Mohawk Helicopter unit.

Although Mr. Fitzgerald's memory about the events surrounding the death of Red is clear and accurate, he cannot always separate his Vietnam trauma from his East Troy trauma. When he gets a panic or anxiety attack, he frequently does not know if it's Vietnam or Divine Word Seminary that makes him tremble.

As far as East Troy is concerned, Mr. Fitzgerald said that he has carried the panic, fear, guilt, and shame mostly alone, just like he did in 1960 with the abuse he suffered from Brother Alphonse Horne and Father Charles Malin. Mr. Fitzgerald confided that he has lost the comfort of his faith.

***

Dick Hahner graduated from the U.S. Army's Officer Candidate School at Ft. Benning, Georgia, as a commissioned 2nd Lieutenant. He served in Vietnam in the 173rd Airborne Brigade, 3rd Battalion. He became platoon leader, company executive officer, and assistant to battalion combat operations. He was awarded the Combat Infantry Badge, Bronze Star, and Air Medal and was promoted to Captain.

After Vietnam, Mr. Hahner worked for the U.S. Bureau of Narcotics and Dangerous Drugs (renamed in 1973 as the Drug Enforcement Administration) as an undercover agent, Resident Agent-in- Charge, Country Attaché, and an Investigation Instructor. Mr. Hahner said he found it hard to recall the events surrounding Kenny's death. Learning about what his classmates remembered jogged his memory.

"Just like Vietnam memories, the days and hours are not there anymore, probably on purpose," Mr. Hahner said. "It takes my friends' memories to bring them back for me."

Hahner made several retreats at the old Divine Word Seminary site. The only buildings still standing were the residency for retired priests and brothers and the vacant nuns' convent. "I slept with the lights on and hated to go down the convent hallway to use the bathroom," Mr. Hahner said. "It was a place of ghosts and goblins. It reminded me of the old dorm. I didn't sleep at night, prayed to Mom and Dad, to Kenneth. I still had fear of his 'ghost' walking the building and grounds…The melancholy of it all persists to this day."

In March 2018, Dick Hahner visited Red's grave accompanied by the cemetery director. Buried next to Red were his father Joseph and his mother Gladys. "The day was typical winter, cold, damp, gray, windy," Mr. Hahner recalled. "Not a person in the cemetery but me and the guide to Kenneth's grave. The silence was suffocating. To my knowledge and cemetery records, no one had visited the family grave sites in decades. I cried inside. I teared outside. I prayed to Kenneth and said: 'I'm here so late in life. Forgive me.'"

Back in his motel room that night, Dick Hahner sat down and wrote a poem. He agreed to allow publication but was quick to point out that he wrote it from the top of his head and that it is an unedited first draft.

DEAR RED

Happy birthday Red,
You're almost sixteen
Alone on your birthday, alone

Remember the gym? Basketball?
You so tall, me quite short
Shooting rims and talking
Outside the March cold

Your gentle smile
Petrified memories
Where was I
When the horror struck?

Where was I?
Asleep at your death
Your curly red hair
Red boy of few words

Secrets so painful

No one heard
Sorry dear classmate
Some fifty years later
The small, red granite headstone
Unvisited, unvisited, in the March cold
You the victim
You the martyr

Me, just me
Crying at your roadside grave
Fifty years later, crying

Truth, still unraveling
Waiting for us
To stitch it together
Bring it to light
So your pain and suffering
Escape out of sight.

A Dick Hahner Photo.

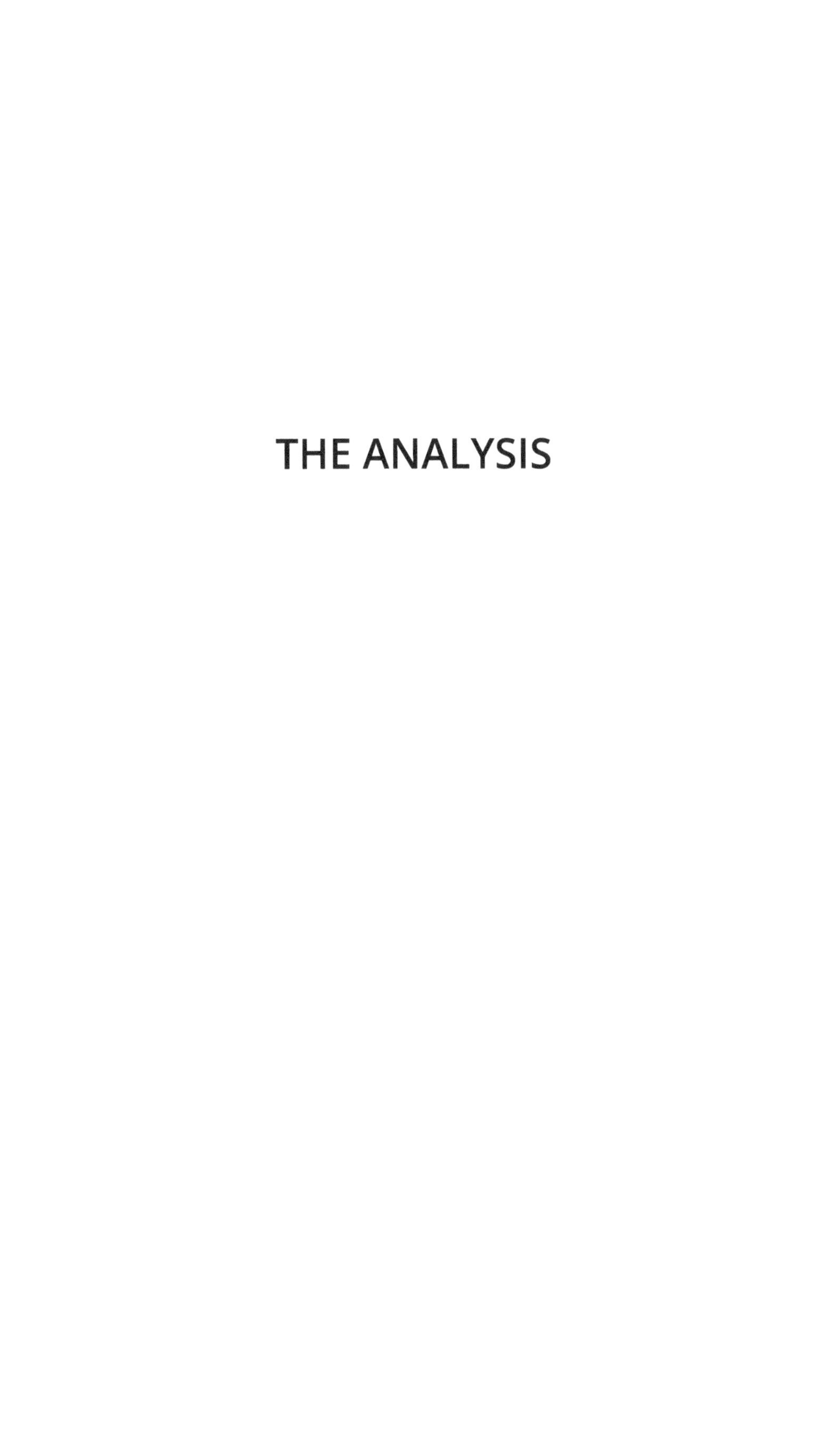

THE ANALYSIS

THE TOUGH QUESTIONS

The year 1960 was both typical and pivotal for Catholics and how non-Catholics viewed them. It was a tug-of-war year between stasis and change. A year of restless preparation for a civil rights revolution for all racial and religious minorities. A year of challenges to the autocratic structure of the Catholic Church, which would culminate in Pope John XXIII's Vatican II upheaval in 1962. That Council opened the windows of the Catholic Church to sunshine, fresh air, new ideas, and hope for far-reaching reform.

In 1960, the Catholic clergy were still sitting on the pedestals fashioned by the faithful. Catholics recognized that their priests had feet of clay and forgave them their sins. To have a priest over for dinner was still a great honor and privilege.

In 1960, more than forty years before the *Boston Globe* exposed the pedophilia cover-up in the Archdiocese of Boston, priests were still universally respected in the broad Judeo-Christian community.

In 1960, the Catholic Church and its priests and bishops were still discriminated against and attacked—even hated. The KKK was still targeting Catholics that year, along with Negroes and Jews—*Koons, Kikes, Katlics*. White American Protestants (WASPS) were still barring Catholics from boardrooms and country clubs. Four months after the death of Red Rudnitski, the Democratic National Convention selected John F. Kennedy as its candidate for president, dragging Rome and the Vatican into the heart of the Bible belt and the political process. Kennedy's Catholicism posed such a threat to his election that he felt compelled to reassure Southerners. In a major speech in Houston, he made it clear to them and the nation that he was no Vatican puppet and that he would never take orders from the Pope.

In 1960, the country was still watching with affection as Father O'Malley (Bing Crosby) and crotchety old Father Fitzgibbon (Barry Fitzgerald) butted heads. The nation listened with delight as O'Malley sang "Going My Way" and smiled as his chorus of delinquent boys sang "Swinging on a Star." Hollywood would not let the nation forget "Going My Way," giving the movie seven Oscars, including one for "Swinging on a Star."

The country still watched with chuckles and smiles as Father O'Malley fenced with iron-willed Sister Mary Benedict (Ingrid Bergman) over how to run a school in "The Bells of St. Mary's"—the sequel to the box office bonanza "Going My Way." And the nation watched in tears when Sister Mary Benedict was ordered to leave St. Mary's school without explanation while the church bells pealed joy and sadness. Hollywood would not let the nation forget "The Bells of St. Mary's," giving the film seven Academy Award nominations and an Oscar for best Sound Recording.

The nation still watched with admiration as Father Flanagan (Spencer Tracy) won an Oscar, shaping and saving the lives of homeless hoodlums like Whitey Marsh (Mickey Rooney) in the Nebraska "Boys Town" he built for them.

And lest we forget: In 1960, the country was still cheering—for one side or the other—as the Fighting Irish of Notre Dame defended the Catholic Church against Protestants like the Mustangs of Southern Methodist.

In 1960, the Catholic Church was still crouched in a defensive stance. The major focus of the theology taught in major seminaries across the country in preparation for ordination to the priesthood was little more than a polemic against Protestants—an exercise proving from the Bible and tradition that Rome was right and still is, and that reformation-rebels like Martin Luther were wrong and still are.

In 1960, on the first day of the new scholastic year, theology professors knelt in sanctuaries across the country and recited an oath against Modernism—a movement that tried to make the Catholic Church more relevant to modern culture. To the Catholic Church in America, Modernism was so dangerous that it bordered on heresy. Two years later, Vatican II would adopt the basic principles of the movement, not that it changed the rigid minds of old-school theology professors who suspected a heretic behind every "liberal" Roman collar.

In 1960, Catholics protected their priests as God's vessels of clay. Although they may have criticized their priests, they rarely spoke ill of them publicly. Nuns went so far as to falsely teach children that it was a sin to say bad things about the good Fathers—even if those bad things were true.

In 1960, Catholic bishops and religious superiors were, for the most part, ignorant about the true nature of pedophilia and the growing body of scientific information about it. They believed that a "pederast" was a homosexual who preferred children. They saw pedophilia as a *moral issue* that could be solved by prayer and discipline. They believed that if they temporarily "shelved" a pedophile-priest in a location without children, he could reflect on his sins and be reassigned to the full ministry after his vacation from children was over. They believed that if they enrolled a pedophile priest in a secret Catholic treatment center run by priests, he would return to the ministry "healed."

***

The job of a historical journalist, who lacks subpoena power granted by local or federal courts, is to pierce the systemic veil of secrecy by: analyzing and challenging old facts and old documents; uncovering new facts and documents, asking provocative questions, challenging the answers; and suggesting logical scenarios to fill holes in the narrative presented in the first section.

The historical journalist's starting point is a question posed on the 1960 Wisconsin State Board of Health Certificate of Death—a question the reader is already asking at this point in *A Boy Named Red*. Was the death of Kenny Rudnitski an "accident, suicide, or homicide?" That question suggests a string of follow-ups.

If Kenneth "Red" Rudnitski committed suicide, did he do so because he suffered a personal teenage angst that he could not handle? Or was he *driven* to take his own young life by a threat or by an act perpetrated by someone else? Or, was Kenny Rudnitski murdered?

If Brother Alphonse Horne was somehow involved in the death of Kenneth Rudnitski, which priests (if any) knew he was a sexual predator? When did they know it?

Did the East Troy Seminary cover up the death of Kenneth Rud-nitski?

If there was a cover up, how high did it go?

If there was a cover up, what possible felony crimes may have been committed under state and federal laws? By whom?

If there was a cover up, which Church canon laws were broken?

If there was a cover up, was Walworth County complicit?

If there was county complicity, how high did it go?

To ask is easy. To shed light is possible. But to answer with clarity, precision, and credibility in a 60-year-old cold case borders on impossible because each answer only leads to another question. As Professor Thomas G. Plante, editor of the anthology *Sin Against the Innocents,* put it:

"Clergy sexual abuse in the Catholic Church is a complex issue with few simple and straight forward answers."

The investigation becomes even more complex when it involves the tragic death of a 15-year-old boy in a Catholic high school seminary with a sexual predator on the loose. Since I have no training in the field of mental health, I can only raise the mental health questions. To help analyze the mental health issues, I have relied heavily on the guidance of professionals, especially a psychiatrist who requested not to be identified for professional and personal security reasons.

***

The analysis begins with Brother Alphonse Horne. Who was he? What motivated him to attack children? How did his superiors handle him once they learned that he was active at Divine Word Seminary, East Troy, Wisconsin, in 1960? How did they react once they learned that he was a suspect in the tragic death of Kenny "Red" Rud-nitski?

THE MAKING OF ALPHONSE HORNE

Peter Edward Horne was born on March 20, 1918 in segregated Augusta, Georgia, the state's second largest city. Unemployment was high, social services limited, and the right to vote virtually non-existent for African Americans.

Peter grew up in an unstable, fragmented family. He had a brother (Joseph) and a sister (Lucy). There were three different fathers. Peter received some grade school education in Sacred Heart Catholic School for Negroes. Although he was smart, his reading and writing skills were limited.

The 1940 census showed 22-year-old Peter living with three Jesuit priests—Fathers Austin Wayne, James Greely, John O'Donahue—in a rectory at 1306 Ellis Street in Old Town Augusta. Peter earned his keep as a janitor for the rectory and as a sextant for Sacred Heart Church. A landmark on nearby Green Street, the church was a towering red-stone structure with huge stained-glass windows and three spires. It looked like a medieval castle. The church closed its massive wooden door in the 1970s; it is currently an Augusta Cultural Center, listed on the National Register of Historic Places.

Peter E. Horne's 1941 draft card showed he was still semi-literate at the age of twenty-three. Some unknown person filled out the card for him. And some unknown person signed his name. Peter merely printed "PETER" in a childlike scrawl next to the signature.

SERIAL NUMBER **3142** — 1. NAME (Print): Peter (First) Edward (Middle) Horne (Last) — ORDER NUMBER **609**

2. ADDRESS (Print): 1306 Ellis St. (Number and street or R. F. D. number) Augusta (Town) Richmond (County) Georgia (State)

3. TELEPHONE: 2-2944 (Exchange) (Number) — 4. AGE IN YEARS: 22 — DATE OF BIRTH: Mar. 20, 1918 (Mo.) (Day) (Yr.) — 5. PLACE OF BIRTH: Augusta (Town or county) Georgia (State or country) — 6. COUNTRY OF CITIZENSHIP: United States

7. NAME OF PERSON WHO WILL ALWAYS KNOW YOUR ADDRESS: Mrs. Fannie (Mr., Mrs., Miss) (First) Colbert (Middle) (Last) — 8. RELATIONSHIP OF THAT PERSON: mother

9. ADDRESS OF THAT PERSON: 1438 Brown St. (Number and street or R. F. D. number) Augusta (Town) Richmond (County) Ga. (State)

10. EMPLOYER'S NAME: Rev. J. E. O'Donohoe S. J.

11. PLACE OF EMPLOYMENT OR BUSINESS: 1306 Ellis St. (Number and street or R. F. D. number) Augusta (Town) Richmond (County) Ga. (State)

I AFFIRM THAT I HAVE VERIFIED ABOVE ANSWERS AND THAT THEY ARE TRUE.

REGISTRATION CARD
D. S. S. Form 1 (over) 16—17305

PETER Edward Horne (Registrant's signature)

Peter enlisted in the segregated U.S. Army in May 1941 (#3402225) eight months before Pearl Harbor. A 1944 hospital medical record indicated that he was treated for astigmatism. It's not clear how he passed his medical. Pre-war eye and teeth exams were rigorous and it's unlikely that an optometrist would miss astigmatism. After the Japanese attacked Pearl Harbor on December 7, 1941, the U.S. Army was in need of millions of soldiers and quickly. By February 1942, it lowered its vision standards to 20/40 with glasses.

According to a medical report, Private 1st Class Peter E. Horne served in an airborne anti-aircraft unit, most likely on a B-24 bomber, piloted by a Tuskegee Airman with an all-Black crew. The B-24's main task was to protect the larger bombers from German Messerschmitt fighters while on their way to deliver their loads. Peter fought in the Pacific for two years, according to a notice in the November 1944 *Augusta Courier*.

Late in life, Brother Alphonse told a priest who visited him while recovering from an operation in a VA Hospital that he was a gunner. There is no reason to doubt the claim. Although a gunner required special training, he was not required to have a high level of literacy.

The rank of Private 1st Class is consistent with the gunner assignment. Horne's military service record would confirm Brother Alphonse's claim, but the record is not available due to the huge backlog of requests from the National Personnel Records Center in St. Louis, in part due to the Covid pandemic.

In August 1944, a year before the Japanese surrendered, the U.S. Army sent Peter Horne to its new Welsh Convalescent Hospital in Daytona Beach, Florida, a rehabilitation and psychiatric facility for soldiers "who lost their capacity to be useful to themselves and to the military service." Half of the solders at the 5,000-bed hospital were orthopedic cases; half were suffering from "mild psychoneuroses" such as debilitating anxiety, obsessive disorders, neurotic depression, hysteria, amnesia, and psychological paralysis. Rehabilitation at Welsh included academic education designed to prepare soldiers for re-entry into civilian life.

The National Archives (NARA), which released Peter E. Horne's Welsh admission card under a Freedom of Information request, indicated that he was "injured in the line of duty," but NARA redacted the name of the "disease" or injury for which he was treated. Brother Alphonse did not show any signs of orthopedic problems. A consulting psychiatrist concluded that Private Peter Horne's "disease" was most probably psychiatric.

Peter received a medical discharge from the U.S. Army at the time he was released from the Rehabilitation Hospital in December 1944, five months before the war ended in Europe and seven months before the Japanese surrendered.

***

According to a *Directory of Membership*, Peter Horne entered the novitiate of the Society of the Divine Word in historic Bay St. Louis Mississippi, in February 1945. The gulf Coast city is 58 miles northeast of New Orleans and a frequent victim of hurricane flooding. Bay St. Louis is also the home-base for the religious order's Southern

Province, which is recognized and respected as the largest and most prolific provider of Black priests and brothers in the U.S.

During his two years as a postulant, Peter Horne would have taken academic classes alongside his religious education. It is unknown, however, whether he received a high school diploma while at Bay St. Louis. In a response to a request for Horne's records, a province administrator said that his file was destroyed during Hurricane Katrina

After completing novitiate in 1947, Peter Horne pronounced the vows of poverty, chastity, and obedience and was accepted into the religious order at the age of 30. He chose the name "Alphonse." In the Society of the Divine Word, Brothers were trained to fill a variety of positions from teacher to bookkeeper, typesetter to mechanic, electrician to carpenter, baker to cook, horticulturalist to farmer, organist to piano teacher.

Newly minted Brother Alphonse was appointed janitor, responsible for cleaning floors and toilets. Although he lived and worked at Bay St. Louis in a sheltered black cocoon, he was introduced to a new and perhaps unexpected form of discrimination. As a brother in a hierarchy of priests, he was treated as a second-class citizen. The discrimination was pervasive and subtle.

In 1970, I directed an international "self-study" of the more than 5,000 members of the religious order. One of the questionnaires used in the study asked the brothers: "Do you feel you are being treated as a second-class member?" The vast majority of the brothers who responded to the questionnaire said "yes."

To be treated as an inferior member in a religious order while assigned to a menial job was bad enough. But once Brother Alphonse left the protection of the Black community in Mississippi and was assigned to cleaning floors as the only Black brother in a string of all-white religious communities, he experienced both subtle and overt racism. In particular, he was treated with contempt and hostility from some of the German priests and brothers who had fought in the during World War I or World War II, and who had embraced Hitler's doctrine of the white Christian super-race supremacy. A student who studied at the East Troy seminary in 1960 found a Nazi flag stashed away in the seminary.

Former East Troy students pointed out in interviews that Brother Alphonse was a loner, different from and avoided by the other brothers, especially by the three German brothers on the seminary staff. It's possible that racism, not suspicion of sexual abuse of students, alienated Brother Alphonse from his "religious community." The racism was a part of a sub-text culture not addressed openly, only in whispers and behind-the-back comments.

As preposterous as the racism allegations might sound, they are based on twelve years of observation and personal experience. As distasteful as it is to talk about those experiences, I feel compelled to provide a few scattered and unrelated examples.

***

When I was in the novitiate, my German novice master, Father Felix Glorius, was an old World War I German Wehrmacht veteran who still spoke with a heavy German accent after thirty years in America. He built his novitiate on an honor system. If you broke a rule, you had to report yourself.

As required, I stood before his table in the dining room after supper and confessed an offense long since forgotten. Seated on a platform and looking down at me, Father Glorius was furious. The rule I broke had somehow challenged his absolute authority. I could see the anger rising in his eyes and his face turning red. When he could finally speak, he said: "You Black Jew. You-You Black Jew."

After I made a presentation to the Superior General and his Council in Rome as the director of the order's self-study research program, I chatted with the Assistant Superior General who was my boss and who had served in World War II in the Wehrmacht Ski Patrol. I told him that I had invited a lay consultant to attend a special training session in Rome for my data collectors from around the world. My boss and I spoke in English.

The consultant, who was Protestant, had a Jewish-sounding name. When my boss, who would soon become a Superior General, heard the name, his face drained white and he slipped into his native German.

"Ein Jude? Ein Jude?"

While I was teacher and assistant prefect from 1963 to 1968, I lived with two old retired German priests who openly exhibited hatred of Jews and who called a Black man "*Schwartze*" with contempt. I found it shocking and avoided those priests as best I could. One of the priests would walk out of the faculty TV room whenever someone turned on the CBS News with Walter Cronkite.

"Jew," he spat over his shoulder as he stomped out of the room. Mr. Cronkite was not Jewish.

***

The racism was not confined to priests and brothers. It extended to students as well. I cannot attest to discrimination at the seminary high school in East Troy, but I can bear witness to the racism at another seminary in the early 1960s.

As assistant prefect, I was co-responsible for the education, health and safety of three Black students who were blood brothers. In an era of segregated schools, the students' parents, whom I met regularly on visiting Sundays, believed that a Catholic college-preparatory school would give their sons the discipline and education they needed to succeed. Over the five years I spent as a teacher and prefect, I never saw or heard of any discrimination against the three Black boys who excelled in academics, sports, and music. And I never had reason to discipline any of them. None of the brothers went on to be ordained priests.

A few years after I left the priesthood, I was invited to attend a senior class reunion. It was both a surprise and honor to be invited and I accepted. I drove from Washington to Akron, Ohio, with one of my former Black students, an attorney. During the long trip, we reminisced about the good old days. At one point, I asked him if the white students had ever discriminated against him. He seemed shocked by my naivety.

"All the time," he said.

THE MISFIT

Brother Alphonse walked into a toxic environment for Blacks when his Provincial Superior, Father Nicholas Bisheimer, reassigned him to the East Troy seminary in late December 1959 when the students were enjoying Christmas vacation.

***

Former students described Brother Alphonse as a loner whom the other brothers (three of whom were German-born) seemed to shun. Were Brother Alphonse's fellow brothers hostile because Alphonse was a suspected predator or because he was a *Schwartze*?

None of the former students brought up a race issue. When they said they feared Brother Alphonse, it was impossible to tell whether they feared him because he was "strange," a suspected predator, or a black man.

Social and behavioral scientists have long since concluded that one's environment influences behavior and motivation. Mental health experts, however, are more cautious about the theory and its consequences. They argue that the environment theory gives victims of racial trauma an excuse not to take responsibility for their own behavior.

Without getting caught in the crossfire of an academic debate, a historical journalist must still ask the tough questions. And the first one is "Why?" After a shocked community learns the details about a mass shooting, it inevitably asks, "What's the motive?" Although the answer doesn't bring back the dead or heal the psychological wounds of the survivors, understanding why plays an important role in the grieving process.

***

Brother Alphonse Horne was born and raised in Jim Crow Georgia. He served in a segregated U.S. Army and worked in a racially painful world as a janitor and second-class member of a religious order.

Two of Brother Alphonse's Provincial superiors found him grumpy, abrasive, distrustful, contemptuous of authority, and evasive. One superior deemed him unfit to deal with the public. This characterization of Brother Alphonse raises two sensitive questions: Was Brother Alphonse Horne motivated to physically and sexually attack boys out of rage? Did he attack white boys because they were white or because they were the only boys available?

I am compelled to raise those loaded questions even though there is no excuse for Brother Alphonse assaulting 13-year-old Tim Fitzgerald and 15-year-old Kenny "Red" Rudnitski. But even a partial answer can help understand why Brother Alphonse committed violent sexual abuse crimes against boys, inflicting lasting trauma and emotional pain.

***

Brother Alphonse crossed sexual boundaries as a predator at the East Troy seminary. Tim Fitzgerald was prepubescent. Red Rudnitski and Bill Burrows were pubescent. Psychologists point out that crossing boundaries indicates a predator driven by eroticism and the need to exert power and feel dominant.

Mental health researchers have also developed a list of characteristics common to pedophiles and sexual predators. The list includes among others: chronic anxiety, insecurity, emotional and social loneliness, low self-esteem, as well as lack of fulfillment, assertiveness, and rewarding adult relationships.

Based on what is known about Brother Alphonse's background, personality, the nature of his predatory behavior, and his history as a serial pedophile and sexual predator those characteristics are an apt description of Alphonse "Peter" Horne. He suffered a lifetime of discrimination, humiliation, and racial hatred. He was a man filled with rage.

ON THE LOOSE

It didn't take Brother Alphonse long to learn school rhythms and routines when the students returned to East Troy in January 1960 after the Christmas break. He began hanging around the darkroom—which was isolated inside his janitorial headquarters—and sexually attacked Tim Fitzgerald there about a month after classes resumed. A week or two later, he hot touched Bill Burrows when he was working alone in the infirmary.

Two former basketball players recalled Alphonse walking into the locker room while they were undressing for a shower after practice and entering the shower room when they were waiting for their turn with a towel wrapped around their waist. For Brother Alphonse to do this was risky and bold since both rooms were off limits for faculty and staff when boys were present. At least five former students recalled Alphonse accosting boys in hallways or in work areas—sometimes too close for comfort—even when other boys were witnesses.

Tim Fitzgerald heard the voices of two people in a bathroom stall on the night of March 7th. One person was definitely Red, the only boy who had left the dormitory at that hour of the night. Fitzgerald saw two pairs of feet in the stall.

Later that same night, Ed Harte caught Brother Alphonse attacking Red on his bed in the dormitory. Finding Brother Alphonse pinning Red to the boy's bed doesn't prove that Brother Alphonse was the second person in the stall with Red. But the timeline strongly suggests it was.

Brother Alphonse took a huge risk when he attacked Red in the dormitory surrounded by sixty sleeping boys. All Red had to do was shout or scream, instead of sob and cry. Furthermore, when Red jumped out of bed and ran barefoot out of the dormitory, Brother Alphonse raced right behind him. Going from a lone student in a secluded darkroom in early February to a dormitory filled with sleeping boys in early March was a giant leap in just one month.

***

No one knows what went on from the time Fitzgerald saw two pairs of feet in the stall at around 10 o'clock to "late night" when Ed Harte saw Brother Alphonse attacking Red in the dormitory. The timeline suggests, however, that Brother Alphonse was playing cat and mouse with Red as he had done with Tim Fitzgerald who recalled Brother Alphonse stalking and terrorizing him.

There are two other giant holes in the timeline. No one knows what happened after Brother Alphonse ran out of the dormitory, except that he was the last person to see Red alive and that Red died around midnight, according to Dr. Ross Baker. And no one knows whether Brother Alphonse was chasing after Red to catch him or whether he was just fleeing the crime scene.

The timeline of trolling, stalking, recruiting and sexual abuse in just two short months demonstrates that Brother Alphonse was a hungry sexual predator who took huge risks. The pattern of abuse—from a lone boy in a darkroom to a boy in a crowded dormitory—suggests that Brother Alphonse was escalating, perhaps out of control.

***

Three former students reported that Brothers Felix and Jude warned them to stay away from Brother Alphonse. Not a single priest who taught, guided, nurtured, and was co-responsible for their safety issued a warning or voiced a concern.

Where were Prefect Father Paul Jacobi, Assistant Prefect Father John McHenry, and Rector Father Charles Malin? Were they so consumed with law and order that they missed the buzz-talk, the tension in the air, the signals of a sexual predator on the loose in their school? Or did they know or suspect they had a "problem" and were trying to pray it away? Were they negligent in their duties?

There are no answers. I decline to speculate.

HIDING ALPHONSE

Provincial Nicholas Bisheimer and Rector Charles Malin faced a problem that could destroy their seminary—a serial sexual predator under their jurisdiction who was the last person to see Kenny "Red" Rudnitski alive. If the Walworth County Prosecutor opened a criminal investigation into Red's suspicious death, it would inevitably lead to Brother Alphonse Horne. He would soon become more than just a person of interest. He would become a prime suspect.

The students' suspicion that Brother Alphonse was somehow involved in Red's death made getting rid of him even more urgent. None of them recalled seeing Alphonse with his mop or hanging around his home base in the basement on March 8th, the day Red's body was discovered and the day the Deputy Sheriff Werner Voegeli arrived at the seminary to investigate Red's death. And none of the former students recalled seeing Alphonse the next day, March 9th. Boys like Dick Hahner and Harry May were asking themselves:

"If Brother Alphonse didn't do anything wrong, why did he run and hide?"

Given the growing suspicion that Brother Alphonse was somehow behind the death of Red, some freshmen and sophomores were so frightened that they had a difficult time falling asleep as long as Brother Alphonse was still on the loose. To find and get rid of Brother Alphonse would go a long way to ease their school-wide anxiety and lessen the risk of leaks to parents about a suspicious religious brother. Some angry mother or father might report him to the police.

***

The chain of command required a Seminary Rector to report all major problems to his provincial superior. Rector Charles Malin moved quickly. He called his provincial superior, Father Nicholas Bisheimer, either before he asked the school's attorney James Voss for help, or as soon as Dr. Ross Baker and Coroner Osmund Bakkom left the seminary late morning after informing Father Malin that 15-year-old Kenneth Rudnitski had committed suicide.

Father Bisheimer's response was clear and decisive—get Alphonse out of there and send him to me. The problem was—Father Malin couldn't find Brother Alphonse.

***

To run and hide is an instinctive act of survival, driven by panic, not logic. It's an almost childlike attempt to avoid being punished. But Brother Alphonse was not a naughty boy. He was a strong, sly, beefy man who had received advanced military combat training, including self-defense and offensive hand-to-hand combat. That made him as dangerous as a cornered Wisconsin bear.

In his panic, Brother Alphonse faced two basic choices. He could try to escape by running through the woods or down the one-mile dirt road to the highway and then keep going. Or he could hide on the seminary grounds. If he chose to run, he had no money, no food, no water, no close friend, no identification, and nowhere to go—except back home to Augusta, Georgia, 900 miles south.

If Brother Alphonse chose to hide on the seminary grounds, it would be easy for Alphonse—the janitor—to find a cranny or a dark hole to hide in. He could choose the school building where it was warm and where there was water and plenty of food in the kitchen pantry. On the other hand, the school building would be the first place Father Malin would search for him. That left Brother Alphonse with two other realistic choices—the boathouse or the farm.

The boathouse was an excellent location. At the bottom of a long steep hill, it sat on the shore of still-frozen Lake Beulah. There was no reason for anyone to visit the boathouse in the winter. No one would even think of looking for him there.

As isolated as it was, the boathouse was also a bad choice. Although it was safe, there was no food and the nighttime temperature was more than chilly. The National Climate Data Center listed the area temperature on March 8, 1960, as 9-27 degrees Fahrenheit.

Alphonse's best choice for a place to hide was the farm. It was distant from the school building. It had a barn stacked with hay where Brother Alphonse could be safe and warm. There was running water and bits of food here and there. If Brother Felix, who disliked Brother Alphonse with a passion, came searching for him, he could burrow under hay or hide behind bales in the loft until Brother Felix left the farm for the day.

***

There are three possible ways that Brother Alphonse could have ended up facing Father Charles Malin, his religious superior. When Father Malin learned from Father Jacobi that Brother Alphonse was somehow implicated in the death of Kenny Rudnitski, he ordered Brother Alphonse to hide in a barn until further notice. Or...Brother Alphonse voluntarily turned himself in to Father Malin. Or...Brother Felix found Brother Alphonse hiding in a barn on that March 10th morning and brought him to Father Malin's office.

Felix had a black steel revolver that he used to slaughter pigs, and Brother Alphonse was beefy, strong, and dangerous. It's more likely than not that Brother Felix delivered Brother Alphonse at gunpoint.

How Father Malin dealt with Brother Alphonse once he had him in his office, was highly predictable based on my eighteen years of experience in the religious order, twelve as a priest. *The following incident is just one example.*

***

When I was a theology student in 1960, the year Red died, one of my friends was accused of sexual assault by a girl who had flirted with him while he was out on a hike. My friend ignored her and kept on walking. When the police notified the seminary Prefect of the allegation, he called my friend into his office and interviewed him with a honey-tongue. After the Prefect got the student's side of the story, he punished him with solitary confinement in his room.

Those of us who knew what had happened were furious. I confronted my Prefect and told him that this is America where you are innocent until proven guilty. I don't have to say that my Prefect was not happy with the confrontation. When the police interviewed the girl, she admitted there was no assault. The Prefect released my friend from "prison."

I only mention this story as an illustration of the typical way a religious superior would deal with a member who embarrassed a seminary in the 1960s. Based on that example and my experience, Father Malin's interview with Brother Alphonse would have been conducted with a spoon of honey and a splash of vinegar.

***

When Brother Felix ushered Brother Alphonse into Father Malin's office, the Seminary Rector already knew that the Walworth County's investigation into the death of Kenny Rudnitski was closed and that Dr. Ross Baker had ruled suicide. Father Malin would be seated behind his desk wearing his best fatherly face while Brother Alphonse stood facing him. Father Malin needed to know *exactly* what Alphonse did to Kenny Rudnitski, if anything, in order to protect the seminary. Too much vinegar wouldn't get the answers he needed.

"Brother Alphonse, I know you did something terribly wrong," Father Malin would say. "But you don't have to be afraid. You're a member of the family. We'll protect you from the police and keep you safe. But only if you level with me and tell me the truth. The whole truth. If you do, you won't be punished. But if you lie, I cannot guarantee that you won't go to jail. So what did you do? Did you sexually assault Kenny Rudnitski? Did you kill him? Were there any witnesses I need to know about?"

As a sexual predator who had been caught before, Brother Alphonse knew that his only punishment would be another lecture to pray and reflect about his sins, another shuffle to an institution without boys, another shelf to sit on and wait for his inevitable day of release. Brother Alphonse had nothing to lose if he told Father Malin the truth—the whole truth.

The regular driver at East Troy was Brother Jude, not Brother Felix. It's clear why Father Malin ordered Brother Felix to drive Alphonse to the provincial headquarters in suburban Chicago and deliver him to the wrath of Father Bisheimer. Brother Alphonse was strong and dangerous. Brother Jude was soft and pudgy. Father Malin needed a big tough man with callouses to subdue Brother Alphonse if needed, and to prevent him from escaping—at gun-point if necessary.

***

After Father Malin sent Alphonse to his Provincial Superior as ordered, Father Bisheimer, "gave" Brother Alphonse to another Province on the East Coast, 700 miles away. With Alphonse out of sight and safely tucked away, the stage was sent for the final step—the erasure of Brother Alphonse Horne.

ERASING ALPHONSE

There is no record in the religious order's *Directory of Members* that Brother Alphonse was *ever* at Divine Word Seminary, East Troy, Wisconsin. Although Father Edward Peklo's history of the seminary lists all the brothers who served there, Brother Alphonse's name was not on his list.

Dick Hahner and Bud May, among others, recalled that the faculty seemed subdued, even depressed, after Red's funeral. Even jolly Jude lost his smile. Several former students also reported that they never heard the seminary staff mention the name "Alphonse" again.

During the summer months, the East Troy seminary molted into "Camp Richard" for boys. The camp went a long way to help pay the seminary bills. Four months after Red's death, I was a counselor at Camp Richard as a theology student on vacation. That 1960 summer, I never even heard a whisper about a Kenneth Rudnitski or a Brother Alphonse Horne from the priests I worked with and met at the camp. Neither did I hear any reference to a boy who had died there in March. In fact, in my 12 years as a priest, five in a high school seminary as an Assistant Prefect and teacher, I never heard of the "suicide" death of Kenny Rudnitski. I first learned of it in 2020 from the men who could not forget it.

***

As we now know with certainty, the Provincial Headquarters outside Chicago kept two types of a files on the members in the Province. There was an archive containing the secret files on problem members and criminals like Brother Alphonse; and there was an archive with general files which contained organizational and biographical information on each member.

A historical researcher, who requested not to be identified, gained access to the general files. To his chagrin, he found them "sanitized." They contained no personal or biographical information. All the researcher found were key dates, such as when the cleric entered the order, in which seminary he had studied, and if a priest, when he was ordained. The record of multiple transfers and reassignments, which would be a clue to "hot potato" priests or brothers like Brother Alphonse, had been "erased."

***

Upon request, the current archivist released the correspondence between Father Charles Malin and his Provincial Superior Father Nicholas Bisheimer for the year 1960. The letters deal with a range of petty issues such as Father Malin's request for money to buy a mimeograph machine, the cancellation of a student track meet, a Mother's Day drive that netted $375, the plan to have a raffle at the end of April, and a heated faculty debate over whether "intellectual students" should be allowed to study unsupervised in the library.

The 1960 correspondence between Fathers Malin and Bisheimer mentions Brothers Felix, Conrad, Simon, Andrew, and Ananias. But there isn't a single reference to a Brother Alphonse. There is also complete silence on the death of Kenneth Rudnitski in the correspondence. In fact, there were only three Malin-Bisheimer letters for the whole traumatic month of March, which included among others: the death of Red; a police investigation; the hiring of an attorney to advise and protect Malin and the seminary; securing silence from the *Milwaukee Journal* and *Sentinel*; Dr. Ross Baker's death certificate ruling of "asphyxiation, hanging, suicide;" an article in the *Janesville Daily Gazette* about the suicide death of Kenneth Rudnitski; Father Malin's role in securing permission to allow Kenny to be buried in a Catholic cemetery; and the strong presence of East Troy priests and students at Kenny's funeral.

Not all of those were so urgent that they had to be handled by phone. Did Fathers Malin and Bisheimer decide not to communicate by letter in order to prevent a paper trail? Were telling letters "erased" along with Brother Alphonse?"

Although the timeline pattern of a silence that protected Brother Alphonse doesn't prove his religious leaders planned a program to erase Alphonse, it strongly suggests that the de facto "erasing" of Alphonse Horne was not purely accidental.

DODGE BALL

THE PARTING OF THE VEIL

In February 2021, *The Chicago Sun Times* introduced a series of articles about Catholic clergy abuse in the Archdiocese of Chicago. Its first news story dealt with Cardinal Blase Cupich's "demand" that religious orders send him the names of their pedophile priests and brothers. The article by Robert Herguth went on to expose the orders that were dodging the Cardinal's mandate. Father Quang Duc Dihn, Provincial of the Chicago Province of the Society of the Divine Word, was on the list of hold-outs. In his defense, he told the *Sun-Times*:

"We are making progress in reviewing files covering seventy-five years, and are now finalizing the list of offenders."

In May 2021, Father Dihn delivered on his promise. He made public the names of thirty-nine priests and brothers who had been "credibly accused of sexual abuse of a minor." The oldest crime was committed in the 1940s. The most recent in 2012.

Inside the U.S., the abuse of minors took place in sixteen different States and the District of Columbia. Outside the U.S., the abuse by predator priests—ordained in the U.S. and assigned to missionary work—took place in: Antigua, Chile, China, East Timor, Ghana, Indonesia, Ireland, Italy, Jamaica, Mexico, Netherlands, Papua New Guinea, Philippines, St. Kitts, and South Africa. The May 14, 2021, headline in the *Sun Times* read:

"Exporting Abusive Priests"

*****

Although the mandated List was brave and welcome, it had major flaws that challenge its credibility. The most glaring weaknesses were the failure to define "credibly accused" and the failure to reveal the criteria used to determine what was credible and what was not. Those two flaws created a loophole. Pedophiles and sexual predators—who might be an embarrassment to the religious order, challenged its integrity, invited lawsuits and expensive settlements, exposed criminal conduct—could be protected by simply determining that the accusations against them were not credible.

The List was incomplete. How incomplete is impossible to determine without studying the unfiltered files on known or suspected pedophiles and sexual predators. For example, The List made no mention of Father Richard Daschbach, a self-admitted pedophile ordained in the U.S. who had a long history of raping minor girls in orphanages in Indonesia and East Timor. His arrest and prosecution made headlines in the Far East.

The List was based on self-policing, a practice that is self-serving and unreliable because it relied on *ispe dixit* proof: "What I reported is true because I said so."

The List also failed to reveal who compiled it and who reviewed the accusatory documents used to determine if the subject was "credibly accused." As the same time, The List failed to reveal whether outsider experts were consulted in compiling and challenging it.

Of special interest is that the statute of limitations had expired on every cleric named in The List. That insured that none of the pedophiles and sexual predators on it could be tried for sexual abuse crimes, and that no law suits could be filed against the religious order or the diocese unless the State in which the crime was committed had extended the life of the statute. A reasonable person might wonder if that was just a coincidence.

The List only held the predator accountable by name. It did not identify the religious superiors who shuffled pedophiles and sexual predators from State to State, Province to Province, County to Country.

The List was deceptive. It made it sound as if credibly accused pedophiles and sexual predators were barred from the ministry, forbidden to wear clerical attire, prohibited from identifying themselves as clerics, and banned from contact with minors. A closer look at the timelines reported in The List told a different story. The case of Father Joseph Fertal is a typical example.

***

According to The List, Father Fertal's first credible sexual abuse of a minor took place in 1968. Instead of being removed from the ministry, he was sent to minister at St. John Brebeuf Catholic Church in Niles, Illinois, where he was credibly accused of abusing a boy. Instead of being removed from the ministry, he was sent to Scranton, Pennsylvania, which was in another Province.

When Father Fertal was credibly accused of abusing a minor in Scranton, he was not removed from the ministry. He was transferred to Corona, California, where the mother of a 16-year-old boy accused Father Fertal of sexually abusing her son in 1995—*twenty-seven years* after his first recorded sexual abuse crime.

According to a report published by Horowitz Law, a firm that specializes in representing survivors of clergy sexual abuse nationwide, the boy's mother had enrolled her son in a catechism class at St. Edward's Church in Corona for "moral guidance." The boy's mother took the Church to court. The suit was settled quietly and Father Fertal faced criminal charges which were eventually dropped.

According to the Horowitz Law report, Father Fertal's superior sent him to a Catholic Church treatment center. After release from the center, he was permanently removed from the ministry and ironically spent the rest of his life in retirement in the seminary where he was living when he committed his first sexual abuse crime in 1968.

***

The List was based on incriminating documents which contain the circumstances of the abuse, a description of abuse, and the names and number of the victims. The List provided none of that fundamental information and the files that contain it remain secret. To be more specific, The List only provides the dates and the years of the credible abuse, along with a mix of generic locations such as Ghana and specific places such as Riverside, California.

The List was as antiseptic as a phone book. It closely guarded the institution and dismissed the victims through silence, arguing that it was protecting their privacy. The List did not invite you to remember the injustice and the pain. It invited you to forget.

THE SHUFFLE AND THE SHELF

In late 1949 or early 1950, three years after Brother Alphonse joined the religious order in Mississippi, he was transferred across province lines to a high school seminary in East Troy, Wisconsin. The records marking Alphonse's new assignment and the reason for it are lost.

Three former East Troy students, who were at the seminary in late 1949 or early 1950, independently recalled Alphonse working at the school as a janitor. I was one of them. Brother Alphonse pulled me into his storage room in the school basement one day and sexually assaulted me. His face was contorted in rage, his eyes burned with hatred.

I have lost all memory of what happened after the assault. But now on nights when my house is silent and my world is quiet and I am restless, I see his face and smell the dank mops, the sweet odor of floor wax, and pungent ammonia. I feel a chill and a shiver.

One day, Brother Alphonse simply vanished. The *Directory* placed him back at Bay St. Louis for the next six years.

In 1957, Brother Alphonse was transferred again. This time it was to Riverside, California, sixty miles east of Los Angeles where the order staffed another high school seminary.

In 1958, Brother Alphonse was shelved in an empty seminary in Iowa. When the school began extensive renovation and expansion in 1959, his Provincial Superior reassigned him to East Troy, Wisconsin. Nine weeks later, after the death of Kenny "Red" Rudnitski, he was shuffled to Washington, D.C., in another Province 700 miles away. This time it was to Divine Word College, a residence for priests and brothers who studied at Catholic University just across the Michigan Avenue Bridge that spanned the railroad tracks to Baltimore.

A Dick Hahner Photo.

Brother Alphonse worked as a residence janitor and kitchen aide for three years before being transferred once again—to an institution without boys in rural New York. After a year of prayer, reflection, and repentance, he was recalled to Washington where he remained for thirteen years. Then, in 1978, he was sent back to the institution in New York for another year of prayer, reflection, and repentance. In 1979, he was reassigned to Washington where he resided for eleven more years.

Brother Alphonse died in December, 1991, at the age of 74 from complications due to diabetes. He had sexually preyed on Washington, D.C. children on and off for thirty years. The details of his abuse—who, what, where, when, and how many—are still buried in secret files. The college residence sat on a hill overlooking a park where children played tag and climbed around on an old fire truck, where teenage boys played softball, touch football, and tennis.

A Richard Rashke Photo.

The pattern of transfers and shelving across provincial territorial lines—from Mississippi to Wisconsin, from Wisconsin back to Mississippi, from Mississippi to California, from California to Iowa, from Iowa back to Wisconsin, from Wisconsin to Washington, and back and forth from Washington to rural New York—speaks for itself.

***

Brother Alphonse wasn't the only pedophile or sexual predator who had been shuffled and shelved in Washington. According to The List, there were four more. One was Brother Camillus Turkilj who managed the kitchen at the East Troy seminary when I was a student there. He groped me in the pantry and was soon shuffled out and ended up in Washington where he became Brother Alphonse's kitchen boss. Another sexual predator on The List was Father Jacque Nyssen. According to The List, he abused children in Ghana in the 1960s.

I knew Father Nyssen well. He was a sociologist on my international self-study team, a gregarious, likable priest. As a sexual predator, he covered his tracks like a pro. He let it be known that he was gay and went to gay bars on weekends with more than a dozen priests living at the college. When I began researching a series on gay priests for the *National Catholic Reporter*, Father Nyssen was my bar guide. He was also the rector at Divine Word College and Brother Alphonse's religious superior during the time Brother Alphonse was abusing boys.

I became suspicious of Father Nyssen late one morning in the early 1970s, when I saw a Black teenager step out of his office. Seemingly undisturbed, the boy walked out of the building onto Michigan Avenue. My antenna went up. But I had no proof.

In 1982, Father Nyssen was assigned to minster in Basseterre, St. Kitts. Once again, he made The List as a credibly accused sexual predator. The List entry simply read: "Caribbean/1980s/ St. Kitts."

***

The country to country shuffling and shelving raises a sensitive question. Did it go all the way to the top? Did Rome—the religious order's Superior General and his Council—know about the systemic pedophile shuffling and shelving?

A VIEW FROM THE TOP

Like the Catholic Church itself, the Society of the Divine Word was an aristocracy in 1960. It was built on the foundation of top-down management and strict rules of accountability. Priests and Brothers were accountable to a Rector or Regional Superior, who was accountable to a Provincial. Provincials were accountable to the Superior General in Rome, who was accountable to the General Chapter of Provincials who elected them.

Rectors have no authority in the autocracy to transfer the members under his jurisdiction to another institution within the Province; only Provincials can do that. With a nod from Rome, Provincials can also "give" a member to another Province. But *only Rome* (the Superior General) can transfer a member from country to country.

***

The U.S. List of pedophile and sexual predators noted *forty-four* country to country transfers. The pattern is both predictable and familiar. In each of the forty-four cases, a priest or brother, who was credibly accused of sexually abusing a minor, is shuffled to another country. Father Nyssen serves as a good example.

Father Nyssen was ordained in the Netherlands. Rome assigned him to minister in Ghana, where he began to sexually abuse minors, according to The List. In his request to Rome to transfer Father Nyssen out of Ghana, his Provincial or religious superior was expected or required to give a reason for his request.

Rome sent Father Nyssen back to the Netherlands. Then, in the mid-1970s, Rome sent Father Nyssen to the Washington, D.C. residence. Finally, in 1982, Rome assigned Father Nyssen to St. Kitts, where he was once again credibly accused of sexually abusing children.

***

The unmistakable pattern poses an unfortunate problem. I could not find any documentary evidence that the Superior General knew that the priests and brothers involved in his forty-four country to country transfers were pedophiles and sexual predators. Neither could I locate an insider who could confirm that Rome knew.

The only way to learn the truth would be either to criminally charge individual priests at the top and subpoena all relevant secret documents, or to file a civil suit against the religious order and subpoena the relevant secret documents. Although anything is possible, the waters are uncharted. All attempts to hold Rome accountable to date have failed.

The only applicable standard is: What would a reasonable person conclude from the top-down, country to country transfers of credibly accused pedophiles and sexual predators?

NEED-TO-KNOW

Throughout the centuries, dictators, oligarchs, aristocrats, democratic governments, intelligence agencies, and criminal organizations have used a common-sense strategy to protect their closely guarded secrets—the "need to know" chain of command. Rome, dioceses, and religious orders used the "need to know" principle to assure law and order within, and to insulate and protect themselves from bad publicity, lawsuits, and criminal charges. At the heart of the need-to-know system are the secret files.

***

There are three little known canons in church law that specifically deal with secret information (489, 490, and 1719.) These canons order Bishops to maintain what they call "secret files" which should be labeled "Conscience Files" or something similar. Religious orders, like Bishops, are bound by the dictates of Church Canon Law.

The Canon Laws describe how Bishops and Religious Superiors are to maintain and curate those files. They must be kept: "In a secure place which is either separate from the other archives, or if this is not possible, in a place in the diocesan archives, which is secure. Only the bishop is to have the key to the secret files."

The canons go on to detail what kind of secrets are to be kept in the "secret files." High on the list are "sex abuse or sexual misconduct." The canons do not specify that the Bishops have the obligation to report pedophiles and sexual predators to the police. To the contrary, Church Law clearly states that Bishops do not have to report to anyone but the Papal Delegate who resides in Washington, D.C.

***

The pedophile and sexual predator secret files in Society of the Divine Word in 1960 were shared on a need-to-know basis. I have uncovered no evidence that the order's Provincials were on the

Superior General's need-to-know list. Whether he told them that the Priest or Brother he was assigning to their Province was a pedophile or a sexual predator is open to speculation.

After the Superior General, the Provincials, who were the guardians of secret files, were next in the power chain. If a Provincial knew that a Priest or Brother whom he was "giving" to another province was a pedophile or sexual-predator, he would be morally obligated to warn the receiving Provincial. It's not clear whether he was required to issue a "buyer beware" every time he made a cross-province shuffle.

There is documentary evidence that some Bishops were so eager to get rid of sexual offending priests, they gave them to another Bishop without full disclosure. Boston's Cardinal Law is a good example. In 1990, he "gave" Father Paul Shanley—an entrenched sexual predator—to the Diocese of San Bernardino without warning the Bishop.

Father Shanley served at St. Ann's Church for three years until he was credibly accused of sexually abusing pubescent boys. He eventually admitted to nine sexual encounters and was sentenced to 12-15 years in prison. Father Shanley was paroled after twelve years. The Archdiocese of Boston quietly settled with several Shanley-victims and the Vatican finally laicized him in 2004.

***

Although Rectors like East Troy's Father Charles Malin were next in the power chain, they *were not* on the need-to-know list, even though they were responsible for the spiritual, physical, and mental health of the members and the children under their jurisdiction. For example, if Provincial Father Bisheimer told Rector Father Malin that Brother Alphonse had a pedophile/sexual predator history, Father Malin could refuse to accept him. In that case, Father Bisheimer could order him to obey since Father Malin had taken the vow of obedience. In that case, he could resign.

If Father Malin learned after the fact that Brother Alphonse was a sexual predator, he could warn the Prefects and thus "out" the secret.

He could go over the head of the Provincial and go to Rome. He could report him to the police. Or, he could remain loyal and silent.

If the Rector was not on the need-to-know list, I, as a mere Assistant Prefect at the bottom of the power chain, certainly was not. As far as sexual abuse secrets go, we Prefects were extremely dangerous. Even though protecting students from harm was not listed on our job descriptions, it was or should have been the concern of every Prefect, every waking hour, of every single day.
I was a victim of the need-to-know-system.

***

When I was appointed assistant prefect at Divine Word Seminary in Girard, Pennsylvania, in 1964, my provincial superior Father Leo Hotze did not tell me there was a sexual predator living and working at the school. Brother Edmond Murphy served as the seminary bookkeeper, and he was a talented pianist who could play any musical composition he heard by ear and in any key. I led the school's music program at the time, and Brother Ed helped me with musical arrangements for the five-piece combo I directed. I never suspected he was a sexual predator.

Several years before I arrived at the seminary, Brother Murphy volunteered as a wrestling coach for a group of Erie boys. During a nude practice, he raped a 16-year-old. The boy told his mother, who made a report to the Bishop of the Diocese of Erie, who informed Father Hotze, who failed to call the police or reassign Brother Edmond to an institution without boys. Edmond remained at the school until it closed in the 1980s, after which he left the religious order.

It is anyone's guess how many boys Brother Edmond Murphy sexually assaulted in the more than twenty years he lived and worked at Divine Word Seminary. The Pennsylvania Grand Jury that investigated clergy sexual abuse of children in the state placed Brother Edmond on its list of pedophiles and sexual predators, but he was not on The List prepared by the religious order.

While working on this book, I learned that Brother Edmond Murphy had sexually assaulted one of my students. I was so devastated that I called him in tears and begged his forgiveness. Now in his mid-70s, he told me there was nothing to forgive. It wasn't my fault. His words of comfort did not ease my feelings of guilt.

***

I have worked with and personally have known dozens of Prefects. I cannot think of one who would keep quiet about a known pedophile or sexual predator in his school. The fact that Brother Alphonse was a secret for sixty years is a testament that the need-to-know system worked and worked effectively from the perspective of the Church.

ABUSING THE POWER

THE BOY WHO KNEW TOO MUCH

Thirteen-year-old Tim Fitzgerald was a dangerous boy who saw and experienced so much that he became a threat to the institution that promised to protect him. On the morning of March 8th, he reported to his Prefect, Father Jacobi, that Brother Alphonse had sexually abused him one month earlier. Tim also reported to Father Jacobi that he saw two pairs of feet in the bathroom stall number around 10:00 PM the previous day. Dr. Ross Baker, who conducted the examination of Red's body, concluded later that March 8th morning that Kenneth Rudnitski died around midnight.

Tim Fitzgerald knew that one person in the stall was Red because he saw Red get out of bed and go to the bathroom around ten o'clock. Red was the only student to leave the dormitory after lights out. Tim reasoned that the second person in the stall could have been an upperclassman; in which case, either the upperclassman was assaulting Red or they were having a mutual-consent tryst. Or, the second person in the stall could be someone other than a student.

Without any specific evidence and guided by fear and panic, Tim concluded that the second person was Brother Alphonse. Tim ran out of the bathroom and jumped back in bed. The next morning after Red's body was discovered by Pat Beckman, Tim told Father Jacobi what he had seen and heard in the bathroom and that he was convinced the second person was Brother Alphonse.

If Tim Fitzgerald ever told the police about Alphonse's sexual abuse, what he had seen and heard in the bathroom at 10 o'clock, and what he suspected, Brother Alphonse would be a person of interest in Walworth County follow-up homicide investigation. The police would want to interview each student, teacher, and staff member, including Brothers Jude and Felix who either knew with certainty or highly suspected that Brother Alphonse was a pedophile/sexual predator.

Besides being sexually attacked by Brother Alphonse, Mr. Fitzgerald also accused Father Malin, who was above suspicion, of sexual abuse. Not a single former student confirmed Mr. Fitzgerald's sexual abuse charge against Rector Father Charles Malin. One student and one fellow priest said they weren't surprised. Given the seriousness of Mr. Fitzgerald's recollections and allegations, I am compelled to ask the question: Is Mr. Tim Fitzgerald credible?

Before I begin an analysis, I have to admit to a bias. When it comes to allegations of sexual abuse, I believe the victim. But I also take pains to investigate what evidence, if any, corroborates the victim's allegations.

***

Tim Fitzgerald *was* a photographer, according to the yearbook. Teddy Brown, who allegedly interrupted Brother Alphonse's attack, also *was* a photographer, according to the year book. (Mr. Brown is dead and could not be interviewed.) Another photographer confirmed that Brother Alphonse had gotten "too close" to at least one other student in the dark room. Tim's bandaged hand is supported by the fact that Dr. Baker had given him codeine only to find out that the boy was allergic to the painkiller.

I find every detail in Mr. Fitzgerald's darkroom account confirmed or realistic. I find no factual errors or contradictions.

The emotional angst after the sexual attack, as described by Mr. Fitzgerald, is consistent with emotions typical of sexual abuse survivors. Tim Fitzgerald reported the assault to Father Jacobi about one month after the fact. He also discussed the assault with his brother. After he left the seminary, he did not report the darkroom assault to the police. This is consistent with the statistical research on male sexual abuse and sexual assault victims. Nine out of ten do not report the crime to authorities. Mr. Fitzgerald did not sue Divine Word Seminary. The first lawsuit against the Church and its leaders occurred in 1983, twenty-three years after Tim Fitzgerald had been assaulted by Brother Alphonse.

There is no apparent motive for Mr. Fitzgerald to lie. If he were lying, why did he just accuse Brother Alphonse of groping him? Why didn't he inflate his story?

Brother Alphonse *was* a pedophile/sexual predator. He is on The List of credibly accused pedophiles and sexual predators. The locations where he abused minors were Riverside, California, in 1958, East Troy in 1960, and Washington, D.C. from 1961 to 1990. The year Tim Fitzgerald reported Brother Alphonse's sexual assault to his prefect Father Paul Jacobi was 1960.

I find Mr. Fitzgerald's charge of sexual abuse by Brother Alphonse Horne to be credible.

***

There are no eyewitnesses to support Mr. Fitzgerald's recollection of two people in the stall on the night Red died. And there is no way to prove that Tim heard two voices coming from the stall and saw two pairs of feet. The details of Mr. Fitzgerald's recollection, however, are factually correct and realistic. If Tim Fitzgerald was out "to get" Alphonse, he could have said that he peeked under the stall partition and saw Alphonse pinning Red to the door, and that he noticed a pair of slippers next to the toilet. He could have described the voices he heard in the stall with greater specificity.

Finally, Tim's emotional response to what he saw and heard—fear and flight—are typical of a sexual abuse victim. The eyewitness testimony of Mr. Harte about Alphonse attacking Red an hour or two after Tim fled the bathroom circumstantially supports Mr. Fitzgerald's account.

I find Mr. Fitzgerald's recollection of two pairs of feet in bathroom stall number two to be credible.

***

The details of Father Malin's repeated sexual abuse of Tim Fitzgerald in his bedroom cannot be confirmed. Although other former students were routinely quizzed about Father Malin, no one offered any information that substantiated Mr. Fitzgerald's account. There is, however, strong interlocking circumstantial evidence to support Tim's charge of criminal sexual abuse of a minor.

Father Malin's grooming of the 14-year-old boy is told in realistic detail, including the fact that Father Malin knew that Tim Fitzgerald was an "orphan" and in need of a strong, gentle father figure. Father Malin's observation that Tim had not yet reached puberty is consistent with Malin's masturbating in front of the boy instead of engaging in more intimate sexual abuse. It is also is consistent with his pre-abuse observation that Tim's soft cheeks indicated he hadn't begun to shave yet.

Mr. Fitzgerald provided the names of three other "Malin boys." He knew that these men would be contacted for interviews because I told him I would do so. Why would he run the risk of providing names if he was lying about Father Malin's sexual abuse?

Finally, in the summer of 1961, when Tim Fitzgerald was a 14-year-old sophomore, Father Malin invited Tim to be his travel companion to a library meeting at a seminary in New Jersey. By all standards of propriety, the invitation was highly suspect. Tim's Prefect, Father Paul Jacobi, who attended the meeting, was upset and shaken when he learned that Father Malin had taken the boy to the conference with him. Father Jacobi's reaction supports the unorthodox and suspicious nature of Malin's invitation. The fact that Father Charles Malin was not on The List is no proof that he was not a sexual predator. It only means that no one had credibly accused him of being a sexual predator.

In the early 1950s, Father Charles Malin was head prefect in a Divine Word Seminary in Pennsylvania. Ed Vargo, who was one of Father Malin's students, supports part of Mr. Fitzgerald's allegations.

"You finally confirmed something in the back of my head about him for nearly 75 years" Mr. Vargo told me, "A sad and pathetic episode that you report.

"Father Malin always looked irreproachable. He was a mystery and held his cards close to his chest. But he had his 'favorite boys.' He'd call some of us in to give work assignments or special duties. His favorites he'd keep for long sessions. Sometimes we could hear laughter, so maybe it was harmless enough.

"One morning before first class, Malin came into the study hall to tell us four guys had just been shipped for breaking bounds, going into town, smoking and drinking. The implication was that they were mixing with the town girls, too. Malin was in near tears. One of the boys was a 'favorite.' Who knows what was really behind that shocking and intimidating morning for us?"

I find Tim Fitzgerald's charge of sexual abuse by Father Malin to be credible.

***

Although Tim Fitzgerald's two charges of sexual abuse and his account of what he saw in the bathroom stall on the evening of March 7, 1960, are credible, Mr. Fitzgerald himself has a credibility problem. He was candid about it and volunteered to take a lie detector test.

In 2017, Mr. Fitzgerald was arrested on marijuana charges in New Buffalo, Michigan. According to Berrien County Court records, on September 15, 2017, he was found guilty of facilitating the growing of 241 marijuana plants, a felony crime. Michigan law permitted growing up to 12 plants for recreational use. He was convicted of possession of 3.6 pounds of marijuana with intent to distribute, also a felony crime. And he was convicted of maintaining "a dwelling that was frequented by persons using controlled substance," which is a misdemeanor.

Mr. Fitzgerald was sentenced to one year in prison. He spent six months behind bars and six months at home with a GPS ankle bracelet or tether. And he was ordered to pay just over $2,000 in fines and court costs.

The Illinois "Committee to Expose Dishonest and Incompetent Judges, Attorneys, and Public Officials" suspended Mr. Fitzgerald's law license for six months on credible assault and battery charges in a domestic dispute. Mr. Fitzgerald's two victims, a man and a woman, did not press criminal charges against him. The Committee lifted Mr. Fitzgerald's suspension in 2021.

A second interviewer asked Mr. Fitzgerald the same questions I did and got the same answers. All the details matched. He answered every question we asked, including questions about his criminal record. He had nothing to gain by lying. We both found Mr. Fitzgerald's recollections credible. I did not think the lie detector test would be necessary.

***

Having addressed the credibility of the allegations themselves, the big question is: How did Rector Father Charles Malin and Prefect Father Paul Jacobi deal with the boy who knew too much and who posed a threat to the seminary, the religious order, the Church, and Father Malin personally?

As described in "Part One," 13-year-old Tim Fitzgerald suffered both a physical and emotional breakdown on the morning Pat Beckman discovered Kenny's body. The collapse was so severe that Father Jacobi had to pick the boy up and carry him to the infirmary. As Mr. Fitzgerald recalled, he was in shock. He had been in the bathroom when Father John McHenry stood on a chair and all but declared that Kenny Rudnitski was dead.

Besides shock, there was guilt. Tim failed to report Brother Alphonse's sexual assault in the darkroom. If he had, maybe Red would still be alive. Furthermore, Tim's fear that Brother Alphonse would attack him again—a common reaction of sexual assault survivors—rose to the level of terror. He believed that Brother Alphonse was involved in Kenny's death and, as Brother Alphonse's piece of unfinished business, he might be next.

After Father Jacobi carried Tim to the infirmary and put him to bed, he gave the boy a sedative to help him sleep. Then he sat by the boy's bedside and prayed the rosary instead of calling a doctor or a psychiatrist and informing Msgr. Diebold, the director of Angel Guardian Orphanage who was responsible for Tim's physical and mental health as a ward of the state. By all medical and psychiatric standards, Tim Fitzgerald had either suffered a complete mental and physical breakdown or was at risk of doing so. As an Assistant Prefect, I knew something about handling disturbed students.

***

One day, I discovered that a student in my freshman Latin class was a devil worshiper. He carried a fishing knife that he liked to flash in a menacing way. The Head Prefect Father Leo Dusheck and I took the knife away from the 13-year-old boy and called in his parents for a conference. Leo suggested they take their son home and get him professional help. They agreed and thanked us.

In another case, a student began to float in and out of amnesia and exhibited confused behavior. Leo and I confined the boy to the infirmary, immediately called in a psychiatrist and phoned the boy's parents who came to get him and bring him home for a rest, tender loving care, and further treatment if necessary.

In yet another case, a sophomore student was toying with hypnotism. He found a highly susceptible freshman and put him under so deeply that he couldn't bring him back. Once again, Leo and I confined the hypnotized boy to the infirmary and called in a psychiatrist, who eventually was able to break the hypnotic spell. It wasn't easy. Once again, the parents were notified and called in for a conference. Their son wanted to stay in school and the parents agreed.

I only bring up these three cases as illustrations of how the responsibilities of Prefects would normally be carried out for the sake of the boy himself, his fellow students, and his family. As untrained counselors, we simply exercised common sense.

None of this happened at Divine Word Seminary, East Troy, Wisconsin, in March 1960. What did happen, defied common sense. The timeline tells the story.

***

Instead of calling the local doctor in East Troy, ten minutes away, Father Jacobi relied on a narcotic to keep the boy calm. As a result, Mr. Fitzgerald's recollection of the days and nights he spent in the infirmary are hazy. Provincial and local officials responded to a request to review the infirmary logs with: "We don't know where they might be."

From the timeline and Mr. Fitzgerald's recollection, we know that Tim was in the infirmary on the afternoon when Father Jacobi announced Kenny's "suicide" and delivered the mandates not to talk about his death or write home about it. Mr. Fitzgerald cannot recall that meeting or those mandates.

On Wednesday, March 10th, Joe Dahlstrom reported to Father Jacobi that he was sick. Jacobi sent him to the dormitory instead of to the infirmary. Why the dormitory instead of the infirmary which would be the normal and logical place for a sick boy to be treated until he was ready to rejoin the other students?

Finally, although Mr. Fitzgerald could not cut through the haze to reveal exactly how long he was confined in the infirmary, he said it was several days and nights. And he recalled with clarity Father Malin's announcement to the students during Saturday night Compline that to spread and listen to rumors about a certain faculty member was the mortal sin of calumny.

The timeline and the recollections of Dahlstrom and Fitzgerald make it clear that Tim Fitzgerald was confined in the infirmary until after the police investigation was completed, after the "suicide" death certificate was submitted by Dr. Baker and approved by County Coroner Bakkom, and after the case was officially closed.

***

Even though the Kenneth Rudnitski case was closed, Tim Fitzgerald was still an eyewitness to the crimes of Brother Alphonse Horne and thus a risk to the seminary. What if Tim told his state-appointed guardian, Msgr. Diebold, about the two sexual predators at East Troy—Brother Alphonse and Father Charles Malin? What if Msg. Diebold also exposed the seminary and Provincial Nicholas Bisheimer and Prefect Paul Jacobi? What if Tim told his mother whom he saw from time to time? The solution was simple.

"They tried to get rid of me," Mr. Fitzgerald recalled.

As Mr. Fitzgerald described it, getting rid of him was a relentless campaign by Fathers Jacobi and Malin to convince the now 14-year-old Tim Fitzgerald that he had no vocation to the priesthood because of "immaturity." The campaign worked. After completing his sophomore year, Tim Fitzgerald did not return to East Troy in the fall.

Brother Alphonse was gone. Tim Fitzgerald was gone. That left eyewitness Ed Harte.

THE BOY WHO SAW TOO MUCH

No one saw what Ed Harte saw in the lowerclassmen's dormitory late night on March 8th, 1960. What he saw was traumatic. What he saw made Ed Harte dangerous. He was the only witness to Brother Alphonse's attack on a sobbing Red Rudnitski. Ed Harte was also the second-last person to see Red alive. And what he witnessed was a panicked classmate running past him barefoot and crying, with Brother Alphonse running behind him. Ed Harte's shock was what mental health professionals call secondary trauma.

Since Mr. Harte's recollection of that assault cannot be independently corroborated, I parsed every detail in Harte's account. Once again, I wish to emphasize that I believe sexual trauma victims. My examination is a search for supportive detail, insight, leads, and clarification. In the case of Ed Harte, there is an impressive list of material circumstantial evidence that supports his recollection.

***

In Mr. Harte's account, Brother Alphonse is a predator caught in the act. Whether his attack on Red Rudnitski in March 1960 was physical, sexual, or both cannot be determined. What has been determined, however, is that Brother Alphonse Horne is named as a sexual predator on The List and that his abuse of a minor took place at Divine Word Seminary, East Troy, Wisconsin, in 1960. The List, however, does not reveal the name or names of Alphonse's 1960 victim or victims.

The timeline partially corroborates Mr. Harte's account. Tim Fitzgerald heard two voices and saw two pairs of feet in bathroom two around 10 PM. He was convinced that the second person in the stall was Brother Alphonse, but there was no evidence to prove his conclusion. Sometime later that night, Mr. Harte saw Brother Alphonse attacking Red in the dormitory. Fitzgerald's and Harte's accounts support each other and are in no way contradictory.

The next morning, Fitzgerald told Father Jacobi what he had seen the previous night. Ed did not. His reason for not doing is totally consistent with his relationship with both Prefects, Father Jacobi and Father McHenry. He didn't trust either priest. It's the same reason Mr. Fitzgerald gave for not reporting Brother Alphonse right after he had been groped in the darkroom a month earlier.

Mr. Harte said he woke up "late night" and heard Red sobbing a few beds down the row. Harte didn't have a wristwatch and there was no wall clock. Pressed for a more specific time, Mr. Harte declined to speculate even though he knew that the time of the assault was important. According to Dr. Baker, Kenny died around midnight. According to the timeline, Harte would have seen the attack between 10:30 and midnight. Those hours fit the common definition of "late night."

Mr. Harte's account is consistent with Mr. Fitzgerald's account. All Mr. Fitzgerald could recall is that Red got out of bed and left the dormitory after 8:45 when the lights went out. Without a wall clock or wristwatch to consult, Fitzgerald estimated around 10 PM. The hour was a calculation of how long he laid in bed, eyes open and unwilling to fall asleep because he was afraid that Brother Alphonse would sneak into the dorm and kill him. When Tim returned to the dormitory, he tried his best to stay awake but fell asleep.

Mr. Harte's description of Brother Alphonse on Red's bed was specific for what he saw and what he did not see. He saw Alphonse pinning Red to the bed with one hand on his shoulder. He saw Alphonse leaning over Red with his face close to Red's ear. It looked as if Alphonse was whispering to Red. Mr. Harte did not see Alphonse's other hand. He did not see Red struggling.

There is nothing inconsistent in that description.

Mr. Harte recalled Brother Alphonse releasing Red as soon as he noticed Harte staring at him. Releasing Red was an appropriate response to suddenly getting caught.

Mr. Harte recalled Red jumping out of bed and running away, sobbing and barefoot. Of the three basic responses to sexual abuse trauma—fight, flee, freeze—Red chose to run. Fleeing is consistent with fear and panic.

Mr. Harte said that Brother Alphonse ran right behind Red. What other realistic choice did Brother Alphonse have? He was at risk. Red might come to his senses and scream or pound on Father McHenry's door, which was near the student bathroom. There was no time to deal with Ed Harte who was strong enough to put up a good fight. And a good fight would probably wake up some students. For Brother Alphonse to flee the scene of the crime was both logical and instinctive.

Ed Harte's response to his secondary trauma of witnessing an attack was also appropriate. He didn't fight or flee. He froze in shock. And because he was in shock, he didn't yell for help or trip Alphonse as he raced right by him.

Mr. Harte's teary recounting of the incident sixty years later is emotionally consistent with what he saw and felt that March night in 1960. He was still suffering from guilt because he did nothing to stop Brother Alphonse. "Why," Mr. Harte kept repeating in tears. "Why?" If he hadn't frozen, Mr. Harte argued, Red might still be alive.

The most telling detail in Mr. Harte's account was seeing Brother Alphonse wearing glasses with thick lenses. Mr. Harte said he cannot erase that image. It keeps coming back.

None of the students who were interviewed recalled Brother Alphonse wearing glasses, much less a pair with thick concave lenses. Furthermore, I've seen Brother Alphonse frequently between 1963 and 1975, when I resigned from the priesthood. I never saw him in glasses.

As a historical journalist, I was troubled by the glasses. Why the thick lenses all of a sudden? The detail was so unique it could go either way. It could mean that Mr. Harte somehow misremembered, which would tarnish his credibility. Or Mr. Harte could be correct, which would all but establish his credibility.

About eighteen months after Mr. Harte first told me about that March 8th night in 1960, I received a copy of Brother Alphonse's August 1944 admission card to Welsh Convalescent Hospital in Daytona Beach, Florida. The card indicated that Private Peter Horne was being treated for astigmatism which causes vision distortion or blurring, especially at night. The disease can be congenital or can develop later in life. There were two treatments for astigmatism—corrective eye surgery or corrective concave lenses.

***

Over the course of many interviews, Mr. Harte never changed a single detail in his account of Alphonse Horne's attack on Kenny "Red" Rudnitski, late night. March 8, 1960. I find Mr. Ed Harte credible.

HOUNDING HARTE

Ed Harte was a unique student at Divine Word Seminary. He spent his freshman year at Marmion Academy located on a 325-acre campus in Aurora, Illinois, thirty miles from the downtown Chicago Loop. *Private School Review,* a publication that evaluated schools, rated Marmion among the top twenty schools in the state of Illinois. The Benedictine monks who ran Marmion tasked their teachers and counselors with a distinctive mission—to shape leaders. Besides the usual rigorous college preparatory curriculum, Marmion Academy offered a special leadership track.

Marmion Academy is important because it helps explain why Edward Harte was deemed a problem at the East Troy Seminary and what happened to him after the death of Kenny Rudnitski. Harte challenged what he considered to be lack of leadership and blatant abuse of power.

***

I asked Ed Harte to compare Marmion to the East Troy seminary. He concluded that the schools had several important things in common other than being Catholic college-prep boarding schools run by priests. Both schools were founded on a specific purpose—to shape leaders and to groom future priests. Both valued their mission of spiritual development; both sought academic excellence; and, both demanded strict discipline. The differences between Marmion and Divine Word Seminary lie in the methods adopted to achieve those goals.

"Marmion is based on respect for authority and authority's respect for the students," Mr. Harte explained. "It is based on trust, and it fostered trust and respect. The superiors sought what was best for you.

"Divine Word Seminary was a dictatorship without student participation. It was not built on trust. It used its power to control, to make students subservient. It created self-doubt and lowered self-image."

Mr. Harte went on to describe Marmion's superiors as "true leaders who trusted the students. Their goal was to help students discover themselves and learn how to look out for the next guy."

By comparison, Mr. Harte said, East Troy superiors lacked both leadership skills and a leadership mindset. They distrusted the students and showed them little respect. Their goal was to shape obedient and loyal priests.

***

Ed Harte's one-year at Marion made life at East Troy difficult. At Marion, he trusted his superiors and looked up to them. At East Troy, he learned to distrust his two Prefects, Fathers Jacobi and McHenry, even though they were priests. Mr. Harte said that to deal with their rule by fear and intimidation, he formed a group called "The Four Hartes." It was a huge mistake. The seminary disciplinary code not only frowned on student cliques in 1960, it saw them as a threat to the administration. A clique could become a hotbed of discontent. Members could begin to question authority. And the discontent and questioning could spread like a virus.

I know about cliques. One of my jobs as an Assistant Prefect was to break them up, along with close personal friendships. I refused to do so unless a clique was an *actual* troublemaker, not a potential troublemaker. Without any special training, my guide was common sense. Teenage boys needed close friends whom they trusted. And learning how to trust is critical in the formation of a teenage boy.

Furthermore, one of the missions of a teacher is to encourage and foster critical thinking, a skill that is the foundation of leadership. With critical thinking in mind, I entered our tiny school in the national forensic competition and developed debate teams. As coach, I made it a point to challenge the logic and relevance of their argument but never to suggest an argument or develop an argument for them as other forensic coaches were doing. I also coached students in another forensic category—extemporaneous speaking, an important leadership skill. Our school with 100 students competed against schools with 1,200 students. Two of my forensic students competed in national finals at Hilton Hotel in Chicago.

Given that only a few of my students would be ordained priests, my goal was to form leaders. I was never told why I was removed as Assistant Prefect after two years; maybe that is why. But far from being upset, I was relieved. The responsibility was a heavy and exhausting weight to carry.

***

The mission of the Four Hartes was based on a value that Marmion Academy instilled in its students—Look out for the next guy. The quartet was concerned about the emotional abuse dished out by Assistant Prefect Father McHenry in particular. He routinely used punishment, threat, and fear to keep the students in line. That included breaking up cliques like the Four Hartes.

"Without question there was a high level of fear and intimidation," Mr. Harte recalled. "There was no one to go to. No ear. No shoulder. No love. No kindness. So I said, 'Let's look out for each other.' We became the Four Hartes to protect ourselves and others."

"Ed was his own guy," Mr. Greg Laka, a quartet member, recalled. "Not someone you want to mess with. Physically strong. Always gave his best. We enjoyed each other's company. We had a bond, shared thoughts with one another."

The friction between Four Hartes and Father McHenry came to a head one day after Red's death when a student left McHenry's office sobbing and shaking. The Four Hartes comforted the boy and told him they would watch out for him, protect him. The incident did not go by unnoticed. McHenry called the Four Hartes into his office for a showdown.

"So you're the Gang of Four," Father McHenry told the boys. "You're the Four Asses."

Father McHenry went on to order the boys to break up or else. He left "or else" dangling. After McHenry finished his "furious" rant, according to Mr. Harte, he ordered three of the boys to leave his office. He ordered Harte to stay.

"McHenry stood me in front of his desk," Harte recalled. "He walked around shouting 'what's wrong with you…I can't figure you out…you're hiding something…what are you hiding…what's your *secret*, Harte?'" Father McHenry finished the session with an order not to talk to any freshman.

When the Four Hartes refused to break up, Father McHenry made it his personal mission to break their leader. He began to call Harte into his office periodically and repeated the rant and the questions. Each session lasted about an hour. Father McHenry's emotional abuse only made Harte stronger and more determined to stand his ground.

Asked why Father McHenry was so hard on him, Mr. Harte said: "He couldn't control me. He couldn't break me. He was afraid of me. He threatened me with: 'You will be my altar boy.' It became clear that he wanted me out, to quit. I thought that maybe he was after me because Alphonse had complained about me."

Asked if the reason why Father McHenry wanted to get rid of him was because Father McHenry knew that he had seen Brother Alphonse attacking Kenny in the dormitory on the night Red died, Mr. Harte said: "I never thought of that. It makes sense."

It was logical for Father Malin to ask Brother Alphonse if anyone saw him attacking Kenny Rudnitski in the darkroom or the dormitory. It would be in Brother Alphonse's interest to name Ed Harte because Brother Alphonse knew Father Malin would find a way to silence the boy.

When Father McHenry failed to break Ed Harte, Father Jacobi took over the hounding of Harte with a play from the good-cop-bad-cop playbook. Mr. Harte recalled that first meeting he had with Father Jacobi who told him:

"I almost came to blows with Father McHenry. I came to the point of almost screaming. I said 'It's not right. Not healthy. Do not go near Ed Harte.'"

Father Jacobi went on to offer a solution. "He suggested I should not return for my junior year," Mr. Harte recalled.

Although Father McHenry left Ed Harte alone, the harassment continued with a new twist. He recruited several upperclassmen to threaten Harte if they saw him talking to a freshman. The student gang actually chased after him. In the end, Fathers Jacobi and McHenry won. Ed Harte did not return to Divine Word Seminary in the fall for his junior year. He enrolled in an Aurora, Illinois, public school which allowed him to skip his junior year. Ed Harte joined the U.S. Marine Corps after graduation.

"I stood tall for me and my fellow students," Mr. Harte recalled with pride, but then quietly added. "I wish I had stood up to Alphonse. Maybe Red would be a priest today, doing good."

***

Three eyewitness—Brother Alphonse Horne, Tim Fitzgerald, Ed Harte—were eliminated: one erased, one gas-lighted out, and one hounded out of the seminary. Granted that the prefects had a reason to "encourage" Fitzgerald and Harte to drop out of the seminary for perceived immaturity and refusal to conform; but, was that their *only motive* for getting rid of the boys? Is it a mere coincidence that Fitzgerald and Harte were also critical eyewitnesses whose testimony could destroy the seminary if they were to tell the police what they knew about Brother Alphonse?

In the case of Ed Harte, I don't believe in coincidence.

THE GAMBLE

The death of Kenny Rudnitski placed the East Troy seminary in the jaws of a vise and it was beginning to feel the pain of the squeeze. The path to relief was to create an official "suicide story," then to keep the story in-house. It wouldn't be a lie. Dr. Baker's death certificate ruled asphyxiation-hanging-suicide. The county coroner, who was up for re-election, concurred. But it wouldn't be the whole truth. There was a sexual predator on the loose, a suspect in the death of Kenny "Red" Rudnitski. The need to control the story and keep it in-house led to a five-pronged damage control program:

> Forbidding the students to talk about the death of their friend and fellow student.
>
> Forbidding the students to write home about it.
>
> Forbidding the students to spread or listen to "rumors" about Brother Alphonse.
>
> Sending a letter to the parents of each student telling them that an emotionally disturbed boy at the seminary had committed suicide.
>
> Weaponizing sin to control the students by threatening them with eternal damnation in hell.

It's unlikely that Fathers Paul Jacobi and Charles Malin sat down and designed the interlocking program after Dr. Ross Baker and Deputy Werner Voegeli left the seminary to report their findings. It's more likely that the program evolved during the Monday through Saturday interval following Red's death.

Once again, there are tough questions that need to be addressed. As outlined in earlier chapters, former students reported various degrees of trauma. Some of it was acute. Did the silence mandate cause the trauma? Did it intensify it and make it worse? Did Fathers Jacobi and Malin place the safety of the seminary before the safety of the students?

As the following alphabetical list of emotions (reported by former students) demonstrates, their trauma was real and far from trivial:

anger, anxiety, confusion, depression, disbelief, fear, grief, guilt, insecurity, loneliness, nightmares, panic, physical illness, sadness, sense of loss, shock, suppression of emotions.

***

Late afternoon on Tuesday March 8th, the day three students discovered Red's body hanging on the clothes hook in the second bathroom stall, Father Jacobi told the students that Kenny Rudnitski had taken his own life. Father Jacobi didn't explain how. He didn't have to. Pat Beckman, Jerome Richter, and Larry Shadegg had spread the news that they found Red dead in the bathroom. His bare feet were blue. Father Jacobi went on to order the students not to talk about the 15-year-old boy's death and not to write home about it.

Coming from the mouth of a priest, Jacobi's orders were more than just the commands of a prefect. According to Mr. Hahner and Mr. May, among others, they were a moral mandate because, they believed, it was a sin to disobey a priest. They suffered pangs of guilt whenever they discussed Red's death among themselves in hushed conversations and huddled whispers.

In effect, Jacobi's two moral imperatives amounted to weaponizing sin, defined as using the threat of sin and divine punishment to achieve a goal. In the case of Red Rudnitski, the goal was to promote the suicide story and keep the full truth of the boy's death in-house where it could be controlled.

***

On Saturday night, five days after Red's death, Father Malin, the Rector and chief authority figure in the seminary, addressed the students, warning them about "rumors" concerning an unnamed member of the staff. The students who were circulating or listening to those "rumors," Father Malin said, knew who he was.

Father Malin went on to warn the boys that it was *calumny* to either spread or listen to those rumors because they destroyed the reputation of an innocent man. Father Malin explained that calumny was a mortal sin. Father Malin lied. He had known for several days, if not earlier, that Brother Alphonse was a sexual predator. He also knew that Brother Alphonse was somehow involved in Red's death. He probably learned the details of Brother Alphonse's crime during his interview with Brother Alphonse before sending him to provincial headquarters just outside Chicago.

Furthermore, Father Malin told the lie to the students gathered in the chapel for Compline, a sacred religious ritual. He was dressed in priestly garments—a purple cope and purple stole. Candles were flickering on the altar. There was the sweet, calming scent of incense. Those religious symbols added weight and legitimacy to his lie. God was his witness. And the lie was baptized in holy water.

It is unlikely that Father Malin deliberately chose the religious ceremony to sanctify his message and his lie. Saturday night was the regular time when a seminary rector delivered a sermon or a religious pep talk. But the end result was still the same. Solemnity with God as Father Malin's witness added a religious aura to the mandate and to the lie.

The descriptions of the emotional impact and degree of trauma in earlier chapters speak for themselves. There was guilt. There were nightmares based on fear of Brother Alphonse. There was depression and shock. There was no one to talk to, especially parents. Any judgment, however, as to whether the mandates had a short term or long term effect on the mental health of individual students, would be pure speculation. The most one can say is that the students suffered "acute stress," according to a consulting psychiatrist, and that the moral mandates intensified the stress and the trauma.

***

After reviewing all the evidence, especially the recollections of former seminary students, and in consultation with a psychiatrist, I have concluded that the damage control program was an orchestrated attempt by men of power to encourage a hundred students to bury their confusion, doubts, grief, anger, and shock. As such, it was a risky, defensive maneuver. It punished boys for the negligence, incompetence, and abuse of power of their adult superiors in order to protect a dangerous, serial sexual predator and the good reputation of a school.

As harsh as it may sound, Divine Word Seminary's loyalty was to Divine Word Seminary. Intensifying the emotional stress and trauma of the students was collateral damage.

THE SYSTEMIC FLAW

FILLING HOLES

How was it possible, even by 1960 standards, that Fathers Paul Jacobi, John McHenry, and Charles Malin failed to recognize that their moral imperatives of silence would intensify student-trauma, and that they were offering angst instead of comfort? Did the legal and public relations consequences of the death of Kenneth "Red" Rudnitski blind them or blur their vision?

To understand how it was possible for three educated and intelligent men to create and enforce a self-serving damage control program at the expense of a hundred innocent and somewhat naive boys, it is vital to know:

1. Who held the power.
2. What qualifications they had to exercise that power.
3. How that power could be abused.
4. Why that power was actually abused.

The three seminary priests comprised the seat of seminary power, which bordered on absolute—Fathers Jacobi, McHenry, and Malin. I dealt with Father Malin in a previous chapter. I deal with Prefects Jacobi and McHenry in this chapter and the next. There is a temptation to evaluate their performance by today's standards. I hope I don't fall into that trap.

***

During my twelve years as a priest, I witnessed the Word and handed down the faith from the pulpit nearly every Sunday. I heard confessions for hours on end and stepped out of the confessional exhausted from the weight of the sins of others. I baptized wailing babies. I married beaming couples. I counseled troubled adults, youths, nuns, and married couples. I served as chaplain to a county home for the aged. I anointed the dying and prayed for them. I sat by their lonely bedside and held their hand as they breathed their last breath. Sometimes it was a peaceful sigh. Sometimes it was a final struggle, especially if they were mothers with young children. I buried them with inadequate words of comfort.

None of those pastoral services weighed more heavily on my soul than serving as a Prefect in a high school seminary. What can be more important than guarding the physical and spiritual health of teenagers? What could be more important than playing a major role in shaping the character and values of future leaders? Some seminary students would eventually become priests and missionaries in Papua New Guinea, Ghana, or on the romantic isle of Bali. Some would teach in universities in Nagoya and Manila. The vast majority would not become priests. A 1975 study calculated that it took 107 high school seminarians to produce a single ordination.

Some would become leaders in the worlds of business, commerce, engineering, real estate, education, and construction management. Some would become officers and platoon leaders in the U.S. Army, Air Force, or Marines in Vietnam. Some would come home with Purple Hearts and Bronze Stars. Some would come home in a casket. Some would suffer post-combat nightmares.

As was common practice in 1960, I had no special training in psychology, counseling, or social work to prepare me for my job as the shepherd of one hundred teenage boys. All I had was four years of bookish theology, two college courses in Education (which were required to receive a Bachelor of Arts degree), and a Roman Collar. The 1960 assumption was that theology and the collar were adequate preparations for the task and privilege of guiding, protecting, and educating boys eager to serve mankind and make a difference. How I got my job as Prefect was typical.

***

One Friday night in September 1963, while I was stationed in Washington, D.C., I got a phone call from my Provincial Superior at ten o'clock at night. I had just crawled into bed, and I answered the hallway phone in my pajamas. The Provincial told me that a lay teacher at the Divine Word Seminary in Girard, Pennsylvania, resigned without warning. My boss ordered me to hop a flight to Erie the next day. As I flew over the Alleghenies and landed at Erie International Airport where a car was waiting for me, I nursed only one emotion—disappointment. I never wanted to be a classroom teacher and I specifically requested a pastoral post.

On Monday morning, two days later, I stepped into a classroom at 8:45. Out of thirty class periods each week, I filled twenty-two. I had to teach five different subjects. On weekends, I served at a local parish, hearing confessions on Saturday afternoon and evening, and celebrating two Masses with homilies on Sunday morning. Sunday evening, I prepared for Monday's classes. I was back in the classroom on Monday at 8:45 still tired from Sunday. I never complained. I did my job as a good priest-soldier as best I could.

One day during a much needed Christmas break when the school was ghostly still and I was exhausted from four months of teaching twenty-two classes a week and pastoring on weekends without a break, the Provincial called me into his office. He told me that the current Prefect and his assistant had been transferred. (I found out later that they were relieved of their duties because they were soft on discipline, law, and order.)

"How would you like to be Assistant Prefect," the provincial asked?

"I welcome the opportunity," I told him without a flicker of hesitation, "but only if you cut the number of classes I teach."

I was so desperate, I would have agreed to milk the Holsteins at five o'clock each morning if he offered relief from my exhausting schedule of teaching and pastoring. The Provincial was apparently prepared for my request. He immediately cut my classes from twenty-two to fourteen. When the students returned from the Christmas break, they were greeted by two new, inexperienced Prefects. Our faces were familiar. We were, and would remain, their teachers as well.

I brought two critical tools with me as I embraced my new job—dedication and common sense. My guide was: "Do no harm."

***

Like me, Fathers Jacobi and McHenry were ill prepared by today's standards to guide and counsel complex teenage boys, help them discover themselves, grow in knowledge, and blossom spiritually and morally. The fact that their Provincial gave them a prefect-coach illustrated the point. The coach was Father Edward "Spike" Dudink, one of my former Prefects. Like me, Father Dudink had no special training for the job when he got the call in the late 1940s. He was a strict disciplinarian, the kind of Prefect his superiors valued. He taught Fathers Jacobi and McHenry the same discipline-system he enforced ten years earlier—demerits for rule infractions, strict silence during silence periods, patrolling study halls, dormitories, and hallways, breaking up cliques and close friendships, and censoring all outgoing mail.

By 1960 standards, our superiors were either not aware or did not care that "Prefect" was a power position open to abuse in the hands of immature, misguided, and insecure men, who could damage trusting boys who revered priests. In 1960, religious superiors didn't believe that some training in psychology and social work was necessary. In fact, too much learning might encourage Prefects to challenge and change the entrenched disciplinary system that had worked for decades.

***

I became an overnight Prefect because there was a hole to fill. I was handy and available. And I was typical. I suspect that if I told my Provincial that I didn't want the job, I would have been ordered to fill in for at least one semester until a replacement could be found. There was a hook buried in that compromise. If I did a good job, there would be no replacement.

Like me, Fathers Jacobi and McHenry were ordered to fill holes. Like me, the 1960 system doomed them to learn from the past and learn-as-you-go. Like me, the 1960 system unwittingly made a false assumption: "You are an anointed priest and therefore you are qualified for the job."

Given the lack of training and no screening, the 1960 prefect-system left the door wide open for abuse of power by priests who were burdened with three competing roles.

MISSION IMPOSSIBLE

According to the 1960 East Troy seminary yearbook, a Prefect was "House Counselor and Disciplinarian." Since Father Jacobi was a yearbook advisor with censorship privileges, he obviously approved of the definition even if he hadn't supplied it himself.

Ernest Brandewie, Professor Emeritus of Sociology and Anthropology at Indiana University South Bend and a former priest with whom I studied was commissioned to write a history of the missionary order in the United States. In his book, *In the Light of the Word* (approved by the order), Dr. Brandewie defined the job of a Prefect in a high school seminary as "testing the vocation" of each student. Under the high school seminary system, if a student could not obey or consistently challenged and resisted authority, he did not have a vocation, which was founded on obedience.

Those three 1960 demands—counseling, disciplining, and vocation evaluation—were competing goals, impossible to reconcile. They forced a Prefect to choose. To expect a Prefect to navigate within those demands was to guarantee confusion and invite abuse of power. To impose them was a systemic flaw.

As a Prefect, I refused to evaluate the "vocation" of teen-age students as young as 13-years-old. A vocation evaluation, I believed, was not only premature, it was presumptuous and unfair. Other than outright disruption and criminal activity, my only evaluation was academic. Is this particular student capable of handling the demanding college preparatory school curriculum? Is a graduating senior capable of managing the equally challenging seminary college curriculum?

***

Fathers Jacobi and McHenry had to walk the tightrope of those three competing roles of disciplinarian, counselor, and vocation-tester. How they managed that would define the character and soul of the seminary. Counseling is built on trust. Disciplining is built on threat and fear. Counseling offers help, resolution, clarity, and peace of mind. Disciplining metes out either punishment or promise of punishment. Counseling is built on honesty, openness and a genuine concern, and empathetic evaluation of the boy being counseled. Disciplining demands unquestioning obedience based on "Father knows best."

It is easy for a counselor, a disciplinarian and a vocation evaluator to cross an ethical line in the sand of morality. I have seen superiors use what they learned in a counseling session to control and manipulate the counselee. When the counselee discovers the manipulation, it leads to cynicism and severs the bond of trust. Lack of trust is a poison in a closed autocratic system.

Not only does the triple role make Perfecting an impossible job, it also confuses the students. It is clear whom they should fear and why. It is not clear whom to trust. In the end, the system encouraged the students to trust neither Prefect. That is what Ed Harte did, trusting neither. In my experience, students seek guidance and help from their Prefects only when they are already deeply troubled and desperate. That is what Tim Fitzgerald did.

***

During my tenure as Assistant Prefect, I can recall only three instances of a student who came to me for counseling. Each of these students was deeply troubled. Thirteen-year-old Tom came to me crying and shaking one afternoon. He had just discovered the body of a dead hobo who lived in a camp next to the railroad tracks behind the seminary. The men selected that spot because every evening, the nuns who ran the kitchen gave them a hot meal; I used to watch them filing across the football field to the back door where a sister was waiting.

Naturally, we ruled the railroad tracks out of bounds and dangerous for our students. Tom broke the rule. Not only was he suffering from secondary trauma, he was also afraid of how severely I would punish him for breaking a rule. My only concern was to deal with his shock and guilt. I assured him that I would not punish him and that I would take care of the police. And I thanked him for telling me. My superior and I convinced the police not to interview Tom. We assured them that the boy did not touch the body, that he was too frightened to do so. Tom was in my daily Latin class. Over the next few weeks, I closely watched him for signs of after trauma shock—difficulty concentrating in class, grades slipping, late or sloppy homework, tears coming from nowhere. Tom appeared to have adjusted well.

The second boy—I have forgotten his name—had just finished reading Ayn Rand's novel, *Fountainhead.* The book had moved him so deeply that he was having a crisis of faith. He doubted the existence of God. I told him that I admired his curiosity. We shared ideas about God and religion, but it was clear that his mind was made up. A few weeks later, he withdrew from the seminary and returned home.

The third boy was 14-years-old and was troubled because he was masturbating five times a day. He was worried that what he was doing was abnormal. To be honest, I did not know if that frequency was/is abnormal. All I could do was not to make him feel more guilty. A vocation-testing Prefect would probably counsel the boy to drop out because he clearly did not have a vocation to the priesthood. The boy did eventually drop out.

I accepted the fact that more students did not come to me for counseling with a degree of sadness. I understood the inherent conflict of the competing roles. I also understood why students saw me primarily as a disciplinarian, not as a counselor.

***

In defense of Fathers Jacobi and McHenry, it was not only unfair to burden them with impossible conflicting roles, it was also dangerous. Sad to say, even by 1960 standards, it didn't have to be that way. The Prefects could have been disciplinarians and another priest on the faculty could have been designated School Counselor. Father Jacobi's and McHenry's superiors did not see it that way. The conflicting roles became useful tools in testing vocations. They gave the Prefect an opportunity to peep into the souls of students. What they saw and learned could help them better control the student and help them determine whether the student had a vocation to the priesthood or not.

***

How did the East Troy *students* deal with the dual roles of their Prefects in 1960? The nicknames they gave Father Jacobi and Father McHenry offer a clue. Jacobi was "Jake the Snake." McHenry was "Mack the Knife."

It is common practice for boarding school boys to assign nicknames to their deans, prefects, headmasters, and teachers. But "snake" and "knife" are both extreme and telling. I asked several former 1960 East Troy students to explain the names. Jake was the "snake", they said, because he silently crept up on students from out of nowhere looking for rule-breakers, especially at night during the "grand silence" which extended from night prayers to breakfast. Father McHenry was the "knife", they said, because he was cold and dangerous.

I personally find "snake" and "knife" indicative of a distrustful culture but worried that I might be reading too much into the nicknames. I asked my former high school seminary student, Duane Dargis, whether the boys had nicknames for me and my associate Leo Dusheck.

Mr. Dargis told me the students simply referred to me by my last name. They called Leo "Deuce." Mr. Dargis was quick to point out that "Deuce" was not disrespectful; it was playful. Mr. Dargis wasn't so kind to "Snake" and "Knife."

"If there was a healthy atmosphere," Mr. Dargis said, "there would not be such negative/diminutive name-assigning. I think the students were walking a fine line in assigning such names to BOTH Prefects. Such nicknames make me question the unhappy and distrustful atmosphere that there must have been within the student body."

***

In 1960, the students seemed to understand the conflict between disciplinarian and counselor. They called Father Jacobi the disciplinarian "Snake," and they called Father Jacobi the "counselor" kind, fatherly, and compassionate. Pat Beckman spoke for most of the students when he said, "I thought Jacobi was a good priest and a good human being."

Father John McHenry did not fare as well. If Father Jacobi was respected, Father McHenry was feared. The best compliment that students offered him was—"I personally didn't have a problem with him." Most of those students were upperclassmen.

The good-cop, bad-cop division of labor made it quite clear that "Mac the Knife" McHenry, ran the school, not his boss Father Jacobi. "Father McHenry was like a Drill Sergeant," Vietnam War Veteran Joe Dahlstrom recalled. "Tough. Bossy. I can't believe this guy was a priest."

A student found a Nazi flag stashed away in the seminary school and pinned it to the wall behind the Prefect table in the dining room before Father McHenry entered. Father McHenry didn't think it was funny.

***

Part of the problem that students had with Father McHenry was that they never knew which man they had to deal with—the controlled priest or the screaming priest. The members of the football team were especially vulnerable to the mercurial temperament of their coach, Mac the Knife.

"I didn't like him," former East Troy football star Pat Beckman said. "I remember him going from calm to shouting. He went up, then down. He had a terrible temper, erratic. I never knew when he would blow."

Those students who were called into Father McHenry's office over a disciplinary issue suffered the most. They feared him because of the emotional abuse he routinely meted out to uncooperative or rule-breaking students. It was not uncommon for a student, especially lowerclassmen, to leave Father McHenry's office in tears.

In Father McHenry's defense, it's important to point out that not only was he ordered to fill a Prefect-hole, he "hated the job", according to a former priest who knew him well. After the tragic death of Red, he was removed from the East Troy seminary and transferred to another high school seminary in Ohio. He was soon relieved of that job and became director of publications, far from high school classrooms. I wrote a couple of pamphlets for him. He seemed contented.

***

In a school atmosphere that tolerated and did not challenge abuse of power, is it any wonder that Fathers Malin, Jacobi, and McHenry abused their power when they created a five-ponged damage control program and covered up the tragic death of Red Rudnitski?

THE ONE-DAY INVESTIGATION

JAMES VOSS

The Set Up

According to the timeline, Father Charles Malin called the seminary's attorney James Voss at approximately 7:50 A.M. on March 8th, about ten minutes after Pat Beckman found Red hanging on a clothes hook in the bathroom stall. Voss didn't waste any time. According to a police report, the Walworth County Sheriff Department's civilian dispatcher, Frank Tooke, received Voss's call at 7:55 A.M. Voss reported that a "man" at Divine Word Seminary in East Troy Township had committed suicide.

Deputy Sheriff Werner Voegeli, who was the detective on duty that morning, reported that he arrived at Divine Word Seminary at 9:15 A.M. According to that timeline, Attorney James Voss had just an hour and twenty minutes to drive fifteen miles from Elkhorn, the County Seat, to the East Troy seminary and interview his client Father Malin. Time was Voss's enemy.

Voss's suicide-call to the county police and his conference with Father Malin were the hasty beginnings of the attorney's defense of Fathers Malin, Prefect Paul Jacobi, Assistant Prefect John McHenry, Provincial Nicholas Bisheimer...and Divine Word Seminary itself.

Since there is no apparent record of that first crucial meeting between Voss and Father Malin, the following analysis is based on established defense attorney procedures as well as facts and clues found in police reports. The scenario was vetted by consulting attorney Helen McGonigle, who considered the scenario typical, logical, and essential to understanding the depth and scope of the cover up of the death of Kenny "Red" Rudnitski.

***

James Voss began his defense in his 7:55 A.M. phone call to the Walworth County Sheriff's office five minutes after Father Malin told him about the death of Kenneth Rudnitski. In that phone call, which was recorded in the police blotter, why did Voss identify Red as a "man"? In fact, Red was a 15-year-old boy. Was it a slip of the tongue? Was it a deliberate attempt to soften the impact of a teenage boy taking his own life? Did dispatcher Frank Tooke make a mistake?

Voss reported to Tooke that Kenny Rudnitski's death was "suicide." Tooke recorded it as such on the police blotter. Designating Kenny's death as a suicide virtually insured that no forensic investigator would be assigned to the case unless Detective Voegeli requested one after viewing the body, examining the bathroom stall, and hearing the conclusions of the examining medical doctor.

How did Voss know Kenneth Rudnitski's death was a suicide, not a homicide? He hadn't seen the body. He wasn't a doctor or a medical examiner. His only source of information was Father Charles Malin. Was Voss deliberately planting a suicide seed in the hope of limiting the investigation?

Having set the stage in favor of the seminary, James Voss's next task as defense attorney was to examine the facts. In order to protect the seminary and the three priests responsible for the health, safety, and education of the students, Voss would need to know the full extent of the seminary's liability. What happened? What were the circumstances? What was the motive?

Voss would have advised Malin that their conversation was covered by attorney-client privilege. There were no federal or Wisconsin State laws in 1960 requiring attorneys to report child abuse or suspected child abuse. Those laws first began to appear in 1962, two years after Red's death. If Father Malin leveled with Voss, he would have told the attorney that Brother Alphonse, a sexual predator, might be a suspect in Kenneth Rudnitski's death and that Brother Alphonse had disappeared or was hiding.

The legal consequences were both obvious and dire. Did Fathers Malin, Jacobi, and McHenry know that Brother Alphonse was a sexual predator before Red's death? If they knew, how could the seminary justify keeping a dangerous criminal on staff? To do so would be a crime.

If Father Malin was totally candid and honest with James Voss and told him about Brother Alphonse, a serial sexual predator, Voss was legally hamstrung. As an attorney, he couldn't ethically advise Father Malin to commit a crime to protect the seminary and Brother Alphonse. Advising a client to lie to the police or hide evidence in a possible murder or manslaughter case would be grounds for disbarment. And it *was* a murder investigation. The police were looking into an unaccompanied violent death. Their job was to collect facts that would help determine whether the death of Kenneth Rudnitski was—as the Wisconsin State death certificate asked—an accident, a suicide, or a homicide.

What attorney James Voss *could* do, however, was to ask pointed questions suggesting that Father Malin might want to engage in a criminal cover up, questions such as:

"Do you realize, Father, that if the police learned that Brother Alphonse was an active pedophile, they will have to consider the boy's death suspicious? A suspicious death would mandate a forensic autopsy.

"Do you understand, Father, that if the forensic pathologist rules that the boy was murdered, Brother Alphonse would be considered a prime suspect?"

Father Malin was bound to get the message and do what he thought was necessary to protect the seminary—even if what he chose to do was criminal. Voss would be in the clear.

After defense attorney James Voss finished interviewing Rector Charles Malin, he would have to build an airtight suicide story with a credible motive for the suicide. Then he would have to coach Fathers Malin, Jacobi, and McHenry on how to present that story to the police. Finally, Voss would have to personally plant the storyline in the mind of the county investigator in charge of the Rudnitski case.

To make the suicide defense work, Voss and the three priests had to agree on the details of the suicide defense, which was crafted to divert the police from pursuing a suspicious death and instigating a full criminal investigation. There could be no contradictions that might encourage the police to doubt suicide as the manner of death. Once the story was agreed upon, James Voss and Father Charles

Malin were ready to face the Walworth County Deputy Sheriff Werner Voegeli.

***

The motive for suicide was the Achilles heel in attorney Voss's suicide defense. If Kenneth Rudnitski was so emotionally disturbed that he chose to die rather than live in emotional pain, why didn't Fathers Jacobi and McHenry spot the boy's angst and do something about it? Why didn't they talk to him? Counsel him? Refer him to a psychiatrist? Call his parents? Those would be the common-sense steps to protect the student from himself. To do nothing would present a strong case for negligence. The Rudnitski family could file charges against Fathers Malin, Jacobi, McHenry, and their Provincial Superior Bisheimer, who had assigned a serial sexual predator to the seminary.

Once the defense story was agreed upon, Voss and Father Malin would be ready to face Investigator Werner Voegeli, examining physician Dr. Ross Baker, and County Coroner Osmund Bakkom in a pre-investigation conference in Father Malin's office. According to criminal investigators, such a conference was premature, suspicious, subject to bias, and a violation of common criminal investigation practice.

After Attorney Voss finished his interview with Father Malin, he would want to interview Fathers Jacobi and McHenry. Voss knew that county police would need to talk to both Prefects about Kenny's state of mind. It was important to the defense strategy to get everyone—Father Malin, Father Jacobi, and Father McHenry—on the same page to tell the same story.

DR. ROSS BAKER

The Elephant in the Room

There are three critical actors in the Walworth County Sheriff's investigation into the death of Kenneth "Red" Rudnitski: Dr. Ross Baker who performed the preliminary examination of Kenny's body and who determined the time, cause, manner, and mode of death; Detective Werner Voegeli who conducted the preliminary county investigation and could challenge Dr. Baker's ruling; and Voegeli's boss Sheriff Joseph Dorr, who was ultimately responsible for that investigation and who could recommend a broad, follow-up criminal investigation of Red's death to the Walworth County Prosecutor.

Of these three, Dr. Baker was the most important player. His decision not to order or request an autopsy was the most critical decision in the entire investigation. Dr. Baker's no-doubt-suicide finding all but blocked a full criminal investigation by the county prosecutor, stigmatized an innocent boy, and denied him a measure of justice. Dr. Baker's no-autopsy decision also insured that those responsible for Red's death and those who covered up the crimes surrounding his death would not be punished.

Five medical professionals and experienced criminal investigators, each of whom reviewed the Voegeli report, concluded that an autopsy was necessary, a total reversal of Dr. Baker's findings. They either found Kenny's death to be suspicious or they concluded that Dr. Baker's ruling, which was based on a five-minute preliminary examination of Kenny's corpse, left questions unanswered and required an autopsy for confirmation of his findings.

Who was Dr. Ross Baker? How did he miss what was obvious to criminal investigators and medical professionals?

***

Dr. Ross Baker was a Catholic who attended St. Peter's Catholic Church in East Troy where he practiced general medicine and surgery. A seminary priest heard confessions at St. Peter's on Saturdays and celebrated Mass with its parishioners on Sundays. Dr. Baker had a close relationship with the seminary itself. Beginning in the late 1940s, he was the medical doctor who treated students and the faculty either in his East Troy office or in the seminary infirmary. Dr. Baker had replaced another Catholic doctor, Timothy O'Leary when he retired. Besides being a Catholic and the Divine Word Seminary doctor, Dr. Baker had another telling tie to the school.

***

Ten years before Red's death on a chilly March night in 1950, I awoke just after midnight to a crackling noise, shouting voices, and sirens. I ran to a dormitory window. The school gymnasium was on fire. Flames were sparking in the midnight sky. Within two hours, the Quonset hut was reduced to a pile of corrugated metal sheets, charred floor tiles, and ashes. All that was left standing was a two-foot high cement block wall sitting on a concrete foundation. The remnant of the fire became our new hockey court.

Two years later, Divine Word Seminary had a new gym with a basement recreation room, music room, and conference room, a new student wing to accommodate the expanding student body, and a string of new classrooms. The new wing was important because the number of students in the old building violated Walworth County fire regulations. The seminary also got a new chapel which was dedicated during a special mass on September 28, 1952.

I mention the fire and the expansion because Divine Word Seminary printed a brochure to commemorate the dedication of the chapel. Tagged at the end of the brochure was a list of financial contributors to the seminary. Dr. Ross Baker was on the list.

Besides being a practicing Catholic, seminary medical doctor, and financial contributor to the school, Dr. Baker was also a member of the Knights of Columbus. With over two million members, the Knights was the largest, most influential and respected lay Catholic organization in America. A seminary priest was the chaplain for Dr. Baker's Elkhorn chapter of the Knights of Columbus. The chaplain opened and closed the meetings with prayer, and conducted religious exercises, special blessings, and masses.

***

In 1960, the Knights of Columbus was under vicious attack by the Ku Klux Klan whose members were afraid that John F. Kennedy might become the next president of the United States. The Klan went so far as to publish a copy of an oath that new Knights were allegedly required to take before being knighted. In taking that oath, the men allegedly professed allegiance to the Pope above allegiance to America.

As Professor Christopher Kaufman documented in his exhaustive study of the Knights of Columbus, *Faith and Fraternalism*, the oath was a fake, propagated through the Bible Belt by the Klan to stoke the fires of anti-Catholicism. It is necessary to set the record straight on the phony oath because the Knights' armor is still tarnished by that hoax.

In 1960, the Knights were loyal Catholics who stood by the Pope, the Church, and its priests. According to Professor Kaufman, however, there was no oath of allegiance to the Vicar of Christ on earth. Furthermore, their guide book, *Charter and Constitutions*, required that immediately after the Chaplain's prayer, the Knights should pledge allegiance to the flag "or other suitable patriotic displays of loyalty" to the United States of America.

***

Given Dr. Baker's interlocking ties to the Catholic Church, one is compelled to ask: Was Dr. Baker biased? If so, did his bias blind him to the elephant in the room? Was his bias so strong that he deliberately buried the truth? Was Dr. Baker willing to risk losing his license to practice medicine and surgery in Wisconsin in order to protect the Catholic Church and the seminary?

If Dr. Baker was biased, was he so biased that he was willing to stigmatize a 15-year-old boy as an emotionally disturbed teenager who committed suicide, which was a violation of the 5th commandment and therefore a mortal sin in the eyes of the 1960 Catholic Church? Was Dr. Baker willing to sacrifice an innocent boy named 'Red' to protect his Church from the devastating consequences of truth and justice?

To put it another way: In the scheme of things lofty, noble, and sacred, wasn't Kenny Rudnitski just a kid who got in the way? A red-headed kid that didn't matter?

***

It's clear that Dr. Ross Baker had a strong motive to block a full criminal investigation into the tragic death of Red Rudnitski and that he had a unique opportunity to do so. It's also clear that Dr. Baker broke the rules of medical protocol by discussing Red's death with Rector Father Malin and his attorney, James Voss, before examining Red's body.

I find that only Dr. Baker himself can answer the troubling question of bias and that the standard for judgment is: What would a reasonable person conclude? I also find that Dr. Ross Baker's preliminary examination of the body of Kenneth Rudnitski was negligent at best.

The Autopsy that Wasn't

Dr. Ross Baker cannot be faulted for giving Red only a five-minute examination before medically closing the case. In 1960, five minutes was typical for a preliminary examination of a corpse, which would determine whether an autopsy was warranted. Dr. Baker concluded an autopsy was not needed. To him, the evidence supporting suicide was clear, convincing, and unquestionable, based on the observation that there were no external signs of struggle or foul play.

An analysis of Dr. Baker's no-autopsy decision raises two fundamental questions. Was Dr. Baker *competent* to make the asphyxiation-hanging-suicide ruling based on a preliminary examination? Did he make any *medical errors* that would challenge his credibility?

The following analysis is based on the medical evaluation of Red's death by Dr. Joseph Hodge, a currently practicing forensic pathologist.

***

Dr. Ross Baker made a judgment call that must have caused great pain for the Rudnitski family. He estimated that it took Red two hours to die of asphyxiation by hanging. It was a guess based on the false assumption that Red would get less and less air, drift in and out of consciousness, then die.

Doctor Hodge concluded: "I believe Dr. Baker's opinion of two hours is an error. Hanging in a position that Red was found in would result in death in minutes. The cause of death is asphyxia due to occlusion of blood vessels in the neck, not airway obstructions as commonly believed."

Dr. Hodge's conclusion is supported by the timeline. If Red died around midnight, as Dr. Baker estimated, then his asphyxia would have started around 10:00 PM. But Ed Harte saw Brother Alphonse assaulting Red in the dormitory late that night, very much alive.

***

One important piece of physical evidence to determine cause, manner, and mode of death is livor mortis which leaves purplish marks on the corpse. Livor patterns and their intensity are like medical fingerprints. Since Red was discovered hanging in the bathroom stall with a handkerchief tied around his neck, for example, the soft cloth would leave an unmistakable purple ligature mark around Red's neck. The question is: Were there other ligature livor marks on the body? Did Dr. Baker remove the handkerchief or move it to expose the neck so he could study the ligature mark?

If Brother Alphonse had choked Red to death, pinched his nose and covered his mouth, put a plastic bag over his head, smothered him with a cloth, strangled him with a rope or chain, or held a choke hold too long, there would have been distinctive livor marks. The ligature mark on Red's neck would have to correlate with the ligature used, as Dr. Hodge pointed out. That comparison is relatively simple to make.

Was Dr. Baker *qualified* to find, read, analyze, and interpret more subtle livor marks or patterns on a corpse during a five-minute preliminary examination? Dr. Hodge did not think so.

"Any physician could determine livor or rigor patterns to make rudimentary determinations regarding time of death and body positioning," Dr. Hodge explained. "External ligature marks could be appreciated by a general practitioner to some degree, but a dissection of the neck by a forensic pathologist would be required. An autopsy would have definitely ruled out the presence of injuries not consistent with a suicide by hanging."

***

Kenny's pajamas were important physical evidence in determining whether he was sexually assaulted. Once again, Dr. Baker cannot be faulted for failing to remove Kenny's pajamas to look for signs of sexual assault or hidden livor patterns that would guide him in determining manner and mode of death and deciding if an autopsy was necessary. If a doctor in 1960 didn't find any evidence indicating or suggesting sexual trauma, he may not have considered the removal of clothes necessary, according to Dr. Hodge.

Dr. Baker did not report any evidence or suspicion of a sexual assault, such as signs of struggle, possible semen stains, or blood stains. If Dr. Baker had found evidence of sexual trauma, he would be required to ask the county coroner to order an autopsy. Without that autopsy or a microscopic and chemical examination of Red's pajamas, there would be no way to determine whether Brother Alphonse had anally raped the boy. If Dr. Baker sent Red's pajamas for analysis, there is no documentary evidence that he did so.

***

An autopsy would begin with a process of elimination. For example, in the death of Red, the examining doctor could immediately rule out death by stabbing, gunshot, and blunt force trauma. A toxicological laboratory would rule out death by poison or drugging. A laboratory examination of the pajamas, a visual examination of the anus for blood and tears, and laboratory tests on swabs taken from the anus and mouth would rule out (or confirm) sexual assault. That leaves the neck.

One of the important bones to carefully examine in the death of Red was the hyoid. Situated in the throat, the hyoid is a mobile, supple, and delicate U-shaped bone which is attached to the throat by strap muscles and ligaments. It supports the tongue, aides in swallowing, keeps air passages open, and prevents choking. In the case of Red, it could confirm whether he actually died by hanging himself with a handkerchief.

"Hanging in the fashion seen in Red's case," Dr. Hodge explained, "where an individual simply leans into a cloth ligature, would not be expected to cause an injury to underlying structures of the neck, such as the thyroid cartilage, hyoid bone, and strap muscles of the neck. The presence of these injuries would imply the possibility of strangulation at the hands of another or, at a minimum, result in a more intensive investigation. Since an autopsy was not performed, one can't say with a 100% certainty that these injuries were *not* present."

DETECTIVE WERNER VOEGELI

The Crime Without a Motive

They still ask: "Why?"

After more than sixty years, Red's classmates and friends *still* ask: "Why?"

So did Detective Werner Voegeli.

If Kenneth Rudnitski committed suicide, he must have had a cogent reason. It's clear from Voegeli's report that he was searching for that reason in his interview(s) with Fathers Jacobi and McHenry, the two priests who knew Kenny best.

***

Fathers Jacobi and McHenry admitted that Kenny used to have a problem. "The Fathers have had numerous conferences with the boy," they told Detective Voegeli. Then they added, "However not recently."

The reason for the "numerous conferences" was that Red had a close friend. The seminary made it a point to break up close friendships, fearing they might be homosexual and become actively homosexual. According to a student who knew about Red's friendship, Father McHenry threatened to expel one of the two boys if they did not immediately terminate the relationship. Father McHenry was so convinced that Red was gay that he called Red a "fruit," according to Kenny's classmate Tom Barry.

Several former students recalled Red crying at night after lights out. Based on Red's calm and cheerful state of mind on the days before and on the night of his death, however, Red showed no signs of grieving or disorientation over the severance of his friendship.

***

Red was not the only one who broke the unspoken rule and had a close friend. Former student David Zork recalled Father Malin calling him into his office and telling him that his friend was "saying bad things about him" behind his back. As Zork explained: Father Malin deliberately turned us against each other.

"I was so naive," Mr. Zork recalled. "I ended up hating my friend."

***

Fathers Jacobi and McHenry went on to tell Detective Voegeli: "No sickness or despondency noted of late. Boy last seen alive at bedtime by the other boys, nothing wrong noted."

The Prefects who monitored the dormitory and the students who lived, worked and studied with Red saw nothing unusual at bedtime. In effect, Fathers Jacobi and McHenry did not offer a clear and cogent motive for suicide.

In reality, Father Jacobi had a powerful motive which explained why Red would take his own life. He did not know that Ed Harte saw Brother Alphonse attacking Red in the dormitory late on the night Red died; but he *did know* that Brother Alphonse was a sexual predator. Earlier that morning, before Detective Voegeli arrived at the school, Tim Fitzgerald had told Father Jacobi that Brother Alphonse had attacked him in the dark room, that he had seen two pairs of feet in bathroom stall number two, and that he was convinced the second person was Brother Alphonse.

In the absence of a clear motive—other than Brother Alphonse—Fathers Jacobi and McHenry went on to suggest one. They said that Kenny was "very nervous and easily upset and shook." They also said that Kenny was worried about his grades. The seminary was a college preparatory school with high academic standards and a curriculum that included four years of Latin, three years of German, and one year of Greek.

"Deceased was a poor student," Fathers Jacobi and McHenry told Detective Voegeli. "He had a difficult time making his grades, poorly talented...Was about third from the bottom of his class of about thirty boys."

Red's former classmates paint a slightly different picture. They described him as a complex teenager, hard to understand. On the one hand, he was likable, fun loving, vibrant with a good sense of humor, easy to be around. On the other hand, he was reserved and reluctant to open up. One of Red's classmates called him an insecure loner, "a roller coaster, up and down."

None of Red's former classmates noted any strong, specific reason for him to commit suicide. That is why they were shocked, and still are, when Father Jacobi told them that Kenny had taken his own life because he was deeply troubled, without telling them why he was troubled. Moreover, they disagreed that Red was a "poor student...poorly talented."

Only one former classmate said that Red was worried about his grades, but he did not think Red was worried enough to commit suicide over them. Not a single classmate interviewed for this book believed that poor grades was a possible reason for Red's "suicide".

"Poor student? No!" Mr. Bob Kairis recalled. "Had to buckle down. Had to work for it. Average. Nothing off the wall. Never saw anything wrong with him. He was a good kid. Normal."

"I remember him as happy-go-lucky," Mr. Bud May recalled. "Not even remotely a poor student. No genius. Totally average. An everyday normal kid. He had a short temper. Got angry fast. I never heard him say 'Oh my God, I'm going to flunk this or that.' I don't recall him as nervous, fidgety, and restless. So alien to the Red I know. A pleasant kid with no attitude. It looks like [Fathers Jacobi and McHenry] were trying to explain things away."

It's clear that Fathers Jacobi and McHenry had a strong, clear motive for suicide—Brother Alphonse—but they did not share it with Detective Werner Voegeli.

***

Father McHenry told Detective Voegeli that he got up around midnight to go to the bathroom. His bedroom had a sink but no toilet. Rather than use the faculty bathroom, Father McHenry chose the student bathroom because it was closer to his bedroom. The faculty bathroom was further down the hallway.

Father McHenry told Detective Voegeli that he saw a pair of bare feet firmly planted on the floor, side by side, and pointing toward the toilet, but he did not ask the boy if he was okay...if he was sick...if he needed help.

Father McHenry went on to say that he entered stall number one, just as Tim Fitzgerald had two hours earlier. Then he peeked under the partition and saw more of the bare feet, just as Tim Fitzgerald had. But unlike Fitzgerald, Father McHenry said he also saw a pair of slippers next to the toilet. He still did not ask the boy in the stall if everything was okay.

To see the slippers, McHenry would have to lie flat on the floor because the distance from the floor to the metal partition was just around twelve inches. If he had lain flat on the floor, he would also have seen Kenny hanging on the clothes hook, as Pat Beckman did later that morning.

As a Prefect, McHenry was responsible for the health and safety of the students. Wouldn't a reasonable person ask: Why wasn't Father John McHenry concerned about a motionless, bare-foot boy standing on a cold terrazzo floor, in March, at midnight? Why didn't he ask if the boy was alright?

***

As Assistant Prefect, I also had a bedroom next to the dormitory with just a sink. There was a common-sense, unwritten rule for seminary staff: do not enter a student bathroom, locker room, or shower room. I never used the student bathroom. Not only was it inappropriate to do so, students might conclude that entering those private spaces was another attempt on the part of the school disciplinarians to spy on them. Furthermore, I find it inconceivable that a Prefect who was responsible for health and safety of the students would not ask the silent, barefoot student in the next stall if he needed help.

Man of Contradiction

If Doctor Ross Baker is a man of compromises, Sgt. Werner Voegeli is a man of contradiction. Unlike Baker, Voegeli was not Catholic. He was a Protestant who was buried in Mt. Pleasant Cemetery in Tibbits, Wisconsin, not far from the Sheriff's Department in Elkhorn. Founded in the mid-1800s by local Congregationalist, Presbyterians, and Methodists, Mt. Pleasant is the resting place for most Wisconsin Voegelis. Catholic or Protestant.

Werner Voegeli poses a problem for an historical investigator. On the one hand, Detective Voegeli was a highly trained graduate from the U.S. Army Counterintelligence School in Baltimore and a certified Walworth County polygraph examiner. He set up and managed the Walworth County's photo lab. He taught basic training classes, including criminal investigation techniques, to police recruits. Yet, he seemed to have failed to notice that the death of Kenneth Rudnitski was suspicious and that there was no clear suicide motive.

On the other hand, given his background, training, and level of responsibility in the Sheriff's Department, it seems highly unlikely that he would put his seventeen-year exemplary career in jeopardy, violate his oath as a police officer to protect the citizens of Walworth County, and commit a felony crime in order to protect a Catholic seminary, its priests and brothers, and the reputation of the Catholic Church. Detective Voegeli's *one-hour* investigation into the death of Kenneth Rudnitski and his subsequent report were superficial and riddled with holes. He was a highly trained criminal investigator; yet, to a reasonable person, he appeared to be incompetent, negligent, and unprofessional.

***

Detective Voegeli participated in a conference with the Seminary Rector Father Charles and his attorney, James Voss, before he viewed the body and the death scene. Such a meeting was unprofessional. It gave the priest and the attorney an opportunity to influence Detective Voegeli, and to compromise his objectivity.

According to forensic pathologist Dr. Joseph Hodge, taking photos of the corpse and the scene in a case of a violent death was a standard procedure, if not a requirement, in 1960. Voegeli's apparent omission to do either is puzzling, given that Voegeli was in charge of the photo lab he set up and managed.

In his short report, Detective Voegeli lumped together his interviews with Fathers Malin, Jacobi, and McHenry. As a result, it's impossible to tell who said what, as well as to determine if their individual story lines sounded rehearsed. Group interviews in a criminal investigation are contrary to established procedures. Besides not calling for an autopsy in his one-and-a-quarter-page report, Sgt. Voegeli did not raise a single doubt or suspicion about what he saw and heard; and, he did not recommend a follow-up criminal investigation.

***

In critiquing Detective Voegeli, one cannot lose sight of the purpose of his report. He was conducting a standard *preliminary* investigation. An analysis of his findings and recommendations had no place in a preliminary report. The investigator was expected to present facts and only the facts.

Although Detective Voegeli committed two errors—failure to provide photos and attendance at a pre-investigation meeting—he did nothing during the course of his preliminary investigation or said nothing in his short report that could be construed as deceitful, grossly negligent, or criminal.

***

Besides the marshaling of the facts, a preliminary investigation has a second, critical function. It lays the groundwork for a *follow-up* criminal investigation by the County Prosecutor. It is the job of the County Sheriff (Dorr), not the investigator (Voegeli), to submit the recommendation for a follow-up investigation. The job of the investigator is to inform the sheriff about his doubts and suspicions, if any, and to tell the Sheriff whether a criminal investigation was warranted, based on the facts and his observations. The important questions, therefore, are?

Did Detective Voegeli tell Sheriff Dorr that the death of Kenneth Rudnitski was suspicious?

Did Voegeli tell Dorr that Dr. Baker should have called for an autopsy?

Did Voegeli recommend a follow-up criminal investigation?

If Voegeli reported all or any of the above, did Sheriff Dorr recommend a criminal investigation to the County Prosecutor?

SHERIFF JOSEPH DORR

Man of Mystery

If Dr. Ross Baker was a man of compromise and Deputy Werner Voegeli was a man of contradiction, Sheriff Joseph A. Dorr was a man of mystery.

***

Joseph Dorr was a former World War I Naval Officer. After an honorable discharge at the end of the war, Dorr spent eight years as a U.S. Treasury Agent chasing white collar crooks. In 1928, he qualified for a full government pension, quit the Treasury Department, and joined the Walworth County Sheriff's department as a motorcycle cop. Nine years later, after serving as a police officer and Deputy Sheriff, he was elected Sheriff for a four-year term, then re-elected in 1957.

Like Dr. Baker, Joseph Dorr was a Catholic who worshiped at St. Patrick's Catholic Church in Elkhorn. He was also a member of the Elkhorn chapter of the Knights of Columbus along with Dr. Baker. And a priest from Divine Word Seminary was his Sheriff Department's Chaplain.

Sheriff Dorr retired in 1962 after forty-one years as a law enforcement officer. Former State Senator William Trinke praised him in a speech at his retirement party: "We all know the tribulations of a Sheriff and a Deputy. Joe has served well, with honor and honesty."

***

In March 1960, two years before Dorr's retirement, Deputy Voegeli presented his boss a no-win dilemma similar to Dr. Baker's. Should he protect the Catholic Church and not question his ace, Sgt. Voegeli? Or should he honor his oath of office to seek justice for the citizens of Walworth County and challenge Dr. Baker's unsuspicious suicide conclusion and his failure to recommend an autopsy?

As Sgt. Voegeli's immediate supervisor, Sheriff Dorr was ultimately responsible for the investigation into the death of Kenneth Rudnitski. As such, he was obligated to read Detective Voegeli's preliminary report, then either approve it and close the case, or refer the case to the County Prosecutor for a full criminal investigation.

A former military officer who was disciplined in the chain of command, Sheriff Dorr understood that the buck stopped at his desk. For that reason, he would have carefully read Sgt. Voegeli's report and Dr. Baker's death certificate, as police protocol required him to do. If Dorr had any questions about Voegeli's preliminary report, he would debrief Voegeli, as protocol demanded, before officially signing off on the case.

Sheriff Dorr most certainly would have questioned Voegeli about what lay buried between the lines of one-page plus report. Dorr would have asked his chief detective whether he had any doubts about Dr. Baker's ruling—asphyxiation, hanging, suicide—before closing the case. Sheriff Dorr would also have questioned Sgt. Voegeli about the lack of motive in the death of Kenneth Rudnitski and would have asked for Voegeli's opinion about the credibility of Fathers Malin, Jacobi, and McHenry.

Given his military and investigation training, I doubt that Officer Voegeli would lie to his superior officer and say that he had *no doubts* that Kenneth Rudnitski had committed suicide. Voegeli was a World War II U.S. Army officer who, like Dorr, respected chain-of-command. He had nothing to gain by lying. He had everything to lose if he were caught lying. In the absence of any internal memos or records dealing with Dorr-Voegeli discussions, it is impossible to prove that Detective Werner Voegeli told his superior officer Sheriff Joseph Dorr the truth: the death of Kenneth Rudnitski was highly suspicious.

A suspicious death determination would have presented Dorr with three choices: close the case and do nothing; refer the case to a County Prosecutor for an aggressive criminal investigation which would include an autopsy and possible criminal charges; or tell

Voegeli to reorganize his brief report, adding personal details and observations, conclusions, and recommendations to the County Prosecutor.

***

If the County Prosecutor decided that crimes may have been committed at East Troy seminary, he most certainly would have handed the case over to the neighboring Waukesha County's Sheriff, Coroner, and Prosecutor. The Walworth County prosecutor simply didn't have the staff to handle a hot-potato-case such as homicide with religious, political, economic, and international implications, leading straight to Rome, the Vatican, and the Pope. Furthermore, the county prosecutor's office had little, if any, experience in pursuing a homicide case. Walworth County reported zero murders in 1960.

Given its limitations, Walworth County had a standing agreement with Waukesha County, the third largest in Wisconsin, to take over big criminal cases. Waukesha's population and tax base was five times greater than Walworth's. Furthermore, Waukesha abutted on Milwaukee County, Wisconsin's largest. The Waukesha County prosecutor enjoyed the luxury of knowing that he or she could call on the Milwaukee PD for assistance.

Sheriff Joseph Dorr raises questions that cut to the heart of this historical investigation into the death of Red Rudnitski:

Did Sheriff Dorr hand over the Rudnitski case to the Walworth County prosecutor?

If not, why not?

If so, what did the Walworth County Prosecutor do with the case?

If nothing, why nothing?

CONCLUSIONS

WALWORTH COUNTY

Requests for information by letter and through a barrage of Freedom of Information requests (FOIs) under Wisconsin State laws and in-person visits, uncovered a distinct pattern of no documents, records destroyed, no records ever made, and "it was a long time ago and we don't know." To be more precise:

The Walworth County Prosecutor's Office reported no records under the search titles: "Kenneth Rudnitski...Divine Word Seminary...Brother Alphonse Horne...Father Charles Malin...Father Paul Jacobi...Father John McHenry."

The Walworth County Medical Examiner's office reported it had no records on Coroner Osmund Bakkom or Dr. Ross Bernard Baker. It had no copy of Bakkom's mandated report or Dr. Baker's notes, if any, detailing his examination of Kenneth Rudnitski's body.

Furthermore, the Walworth County Medical Examiner reported that beginning on January 1, 1961 (ten months after Kenny's death) all coroner reports would be microfilmed. All reports prior to January 1st would be destroyed, which was permissible under Wisconsin State law. Among the documents destroyed was Coroner Bakkom's report. The Medical Examiner's Office also reported that it did not know who requested that Dr. Ross Baker examine Kenneth Rudnitski's body. Other than the fact that Dr. Baker had a family practice in East Troy, the Medical Examiner's office said it knew little about him.

The Wisconsin State Department of Records found nothing, not even a reference to Kenneth Rudnitski. A department spokesperson responded with "Try Walworth County." The Wisconsin State Office of Vital Records found Kenneth Rudnitski's Death Certificate. It provided a copy upon request.

Walworth's partner in high profile cases, neighboring Waukesha County, failed to locate any letters, reports, or references to Divine Word seminary, Brother Alphonse, or Kenneth Rudnitski.

Other than Voegeli's report and a one paragraph entry closing the Rudnitski case, the Walworth County Sheriff's Office said that it did not have any documents dealing with Kenneth Rudnitski, Brother Alphonse Horne, Father Charles Malin, Divine Word Seminary or any staff member. Furthermore, the County Sheriff's Office said it did not have any reports, memos, or references dealing with any communication between Sgt. Voegeli and his superior Sheriff Dorr about the Rudnitski case.

In a word, other than Kenneth's Death Certificate and Officer Voegeli's 1¼ page report, there was nothing, no footprints in the sand, no clues, no traces. There are only questions and suspicions. The consistent pattern of "nothing" does not suggest, however, a county-wide conspiracy to cover up or bury the case of Kenneth Rudnitski.

***

I have concluded that my associates and I did not find any further documents because there were not any. Given the lack of documentation and based on the Detective Voegeli's short report and a Death Certificate, I have concluded that Walworth County conducted a superficial investigation into the death of Kenneth Rudnitski and, as such, was *negligent* in the pursuit of justice. If there were a conspiracy not to challenge Dr. Baker's findings, Coroner Bakkom's ruling, and Detective Voegeli's report, it was a conspiracy of pragmatic silence. Why?

Follow the money.

A focused criminal investigation into the tragic death of Red, which would have included interviews with seminary priests, brothers, and students. Investigators would soon learn that Brother Alphonse was an active sexual predator at the East Troy seminary. A forensic fingerprint analysis of stall number two and the handkerchief, would determine that Brother Alphonse had been in the stall. Investigators would conclude, based on the facts, that he either drove Kenny Rudnitski to commit suicide—a felony crime—or murdered him. DNA analysis did not exist in 1960.

The Wisconsin media would pounce on the story. The national media would cover the story. If Brother Alphonse were found guilty of homicide, the story would become international news. Parents would withdraw their students from the seminary and the school might be forced to close its doors for good. Given the "pedophile" image of the seminary, the highly profitable Camp Richard would suffer low registrations and would likely have to close. The impacts of those realities and probabilities would have dire consequences on the pocketbook of Walworth County.

Besides the loss of tax income flowing from a crippled or dead seminary and Camp Richard, both of whom were major purchasers of county services and goods, there was the summer tourist income. Walworth County has forty-two lakes. It depends on tourism and cottage rentals to support the county. Bad publicity would most certainly deter tourism and dent the county budget.

THE CRIMINAL COVER UP

One of the goals of this re-examination of *A Boy Named Red* is to hold accountable the men who may have been responsible for the death of Kenneth Rudnitski and the subsequent cover up. I developed the following partial list of crimes in consultation with attorneys and criminal investigators. The definition of those crimes that warrant an explanation is based on *Black's Law Dictionary*, a standard reference book for writers and researchers who are not attorneys. Attorneys Helen McGonigle and Bruce Rashke contributed to and vetted the following list of possible crimes.

Crimes Against Children

Negligent Homicide: Death caused by another person's negligence...Father Nicholas Bisheimer for assigning a serial pedophile and sexual predator to a boarding school for children where that pedophile either murdered a child or drove a child to commit suicide.

Reckless Endangerment of Children: Exposing children to physical injury or mental harm... Provincial Father Nicholas Bisheimer for assigning a known pedophile/sexual predator to a boarding school with minor children.

Depraved Indifference: Conduct that lacks regard for the life and safety of another person...Provincial Father Nicholas Bisheimer for assigning a known pedophile/sexual predator to a boarding school with minor children.

Crimes of Obstruction of Justice

Failure to Report a Pedophile/Sexual Predator to Appropriate Authorities: Provincial Father Nicholas Bisheimer, Rector Father Charles Malin, Prefects Father Paul Jacobi, and John McHenry.

Interfering with a police officer in the performance of his or her duties: Rector Father Charles Malin, Prefects Father Paul Jacobi, and John McHenry.

Conspiracy to Obstruct Justice: An agreement of two or more people to commit an unlawful act. The agreement does not have to be formal or in writing. A mutual understanding is sufficient...Rector Father Charles Malin, and Prefects Father Paul Jacobi and John McHenry for agreeing to withhold evidence from a police officer during a possible homicide investigation.

Perjury: Father John McHenry for lying to a police officer who was investigating a possible homicide.

Witness Tampering: Trying to make someone change their evidence or not give evidence...Fathers Paul Jacobi and John McHenry for their attempts to both hide and intimidate eyewitness Tim Fitzgerald and to intimidate eyewitness Ed Harte.

Harboring a Fugitive of Justice: Provincial Father Nicholas Bisheimer for hiding a pedophile/sexual predator criminal.

Conspiracy to Harbor a Fugitive of Justice: Provincial Father Nicholas Bisheimer and Rector Father Charles Malin for collaborating to find and hide a criminal.

Aiding and Abetting a Criminal: Provincial Father Nicholas Bisheimer for providing food and shelter to a pedophile/sexual predator.

***

None of the priests named above were ever charged with the possible crimes attributed to them.

SUICIDE

There were no known eyewitnesses to Red's death. There was no smoking gun. There is only circumstantial evidence. For the sake of clarity, it's important to have a brief look at what the term means and how it is used in criminal cases.

Circumstantial evidence is based on facts, probability, suggestion, and inference. That doesn't mean, however, that circumstantial evidence is weak by definition. On the contrary, prosecutors routinely convict defendants solely on circumstantial evidence. Furthermore, it is considered a legitimate form of proof in both State and Federal courts.

Circumstantial evidence is not considered to be less reliable in the judicial system than direct evidence. In some cases, such as witness identification of a suspect, circumstantial evidence is considered more reliable than the direct evidence of the witness.

To convict a defendant on circumstantial evidence, the reasoning has to be consistent and logical. Prosecutors rely on several elements to make the case, among others: important or weighty evidence; abundance of evidence; a chain of interrelated evidence; and a compelling timeline.

***

What happened to Red in the bathroom stall is unknown. What Red did after he ran out of the dormitory is unknown. What Brother Alphonse did when he exited the dormitory seconds behind Red is unknown.

What is known is: Dr. Ross Baker and Detective Werner Voegeli found no signs of struggle or foul play that would suggest homicide.

What is also known is: The Kenneth Rudnitski's Death Certificate, a still valid legal document protected by law, ruled that Kenneth died of asphyxiation due to hanging and that his death was a suicide. Dr. Ross Baker, who signed the death certificate, ruled out accidental death such as accidental auto-erotic asphyxiation. Forensic pathologist Dr. Joseph Hodge agreed with Dr. Baker.

Since neither Voegeli nor Baker knew about Brother Alphonse, the pertinent unanswered question is: Why?

Why would Kenny Rudnitski take his own life at around midnight on March 8, 1960? Was he suffering a personal problem that was so acute it drove him to suicide? Or was he so panicked and afraid of Brother Alphonse that he took his own life to escape him? Or did Brother Alphonse sexually attack him and he could not live with the shame?

***

According to interviews with Red's classmates and the sworn testimony of Fathers Malin, Jacobi, and McHenry, Red was an intense boy. Months before Red's death, Father Jacobi had several counseling sessions with him. He was emotionally upset because Father Jacobi had broken up his friendship with another student. There were no signs that Red was still upset by the breakup at 8:45 on the evening of March 7, 1960.

Fathers Malin, Jacobi, and McHenry suggested in their sworn testimony that Kenny was struggling with his grades and may have feared being expelled. Interviews with Red's classmates about his classroom performance are inconclusive. They range from normal to average to poor. But there was a consensus among the boys who knew Red best that he worked hard but showed no overt concern about his grades.

Furthermore, Red's friends described his frame of mind during the two days before his death as "normal." He had fun pitching pennies on the sidewalk outside the school building and showed no signs of worry or depression. He shot baskets in the gym with his usual vigor and competitiveness. He goofed around in the recreation room just hours before bedtime. And as Fathers Malin, Jacobi, and McHenry testified under oath, none of the students noted anything unusual in Red's behavior before lights-out. Based on that evidence,

I conclude that Red did not commit suicide because of a personal problem. There was no clear, cogent motive to do so.

Is it likely that Brother Alphonse drove Red to commit suicide?

***

The last known sighting of Red Rudnitski was of him pinned to his bed by Brother Alphonse. Red was sobbing. When Ed Harte interrupted the assault, Red jumped out of bed and ran out of the dormitory, barefoot, and sobbing. Brother Alphonse was running not far behind him.

Red's sobs, panic, and obvious fear of Brother Alphonse were powerful motives for suicide. The Center for Disease Control (CDC) issued a list of seven criteria for determining if a death was self-inflicted. One criterion is especially applicable to Red—"a stressful event."

Besides motive, Red had opportunity. The bathroom stall was right next to the dormitory. It was handy. It had a lock. Red had the means for suicide—his handkerchief. A granny knot is a simple knot to tie.

I've concluded that being driven to suicide by Brother Alphonse is a reasonable and strong explanation for Red's death.

SUICIDE—A SECOND LOOK

There are serious inconsistencies in the suicide scenario. They all hinge on Red's state of mind around midnight on March 8th, 1960. The tears, sobs, and the race to escape Brother Alphonse describe a boy suffering from shock, panic, and fear. He is operating in an irrational mode. All he had to do was scream in the dormitory and his fellow students would have taken care of Brother Alphonse. But he didn't yell. Of these three choices—fight, flight, freeze—he chose to flee.

Once he passed through the double door opening onto the hallway, Red did not pound on Father McHenry's door which was nearby.

Neither did he run down the hallway and beat on the door separating the faculty quarters from the student quarters. He didn't scream or yell for help.

Red chose to run into bathroom stall number two. There are no facts or clues suggesting *when* Red hid in the bathroom. Was it immediate—from his bed to the stall? Or was it later that night? Did Brother Alphonse catch him and threaten him or sexually assault him? Or did Brother Alphonse forget about Red and try to avoid being punished by hiding?

***

Red's mode suddenly shifted from panic to a series of calm, step-by-step reasoned choices. He either entered stall number two, where he had left his handkerchief, with the intention of committing suicide—a rational choice. Or he decided to commit suicide once he was inside the stall and saw the handkerchief—a rational choice.

Red stuffed the door with toilet paper. If it rattled while he was in the throes of death, it might wake up someone like Tim Fitzgerald whose bed was close to the dormitory exit door.

Red wound the handkerchief into a strand, then draped it over his shoulder so the ends of the strand would be within easy reach—rational choices. He tied a simple granny knot, faced the door and attached the noose on the clothes hook—rational choices. Then he either swiveled with his head still in the noose and faced the toilet; or facing the toilet, he reached behind his head and looped the noose over the clothes hook. Then he planted both feet perfectly together and stooped to begin his strangulation.

Red was a panicked teenager of average intelligence. As described, the suicide was methodical and well thought out. The string of rational choices amounts to an interlocking set of material circumstantial evidence, strongly suggesting that Kenneth "Red" Rudnitski was not driven to suicide by Brother Alphonse.

HOMICIDE?

If Red had a clear and cogent motive to kill himself out of fear of Brother Alphonse, Brother Alphonse had an equally clear and cogent motive to silence Red. He was caught assaulting Red and ran out of the dormitory door just feet behind Red. Given those two facts, a reasonable person might conclude that Brother Alphonse was also in a state of panic. If so, was he frightened and panicky enough to deliberately or accidentally kill Red?

I presented the facts of the Rudnitski case as outlined in the Voegeli report and on the death certificate to three criminal investigators, each of whom had more than thirty years of experience. I purposely withheld from two of the investigators any and all information about Brother Alphonse Horne, Timothy Fitzgerald, and Ed Harte. The third investigator knew about them.

***

The first investigator was William "Bill" Taylor. In the name of full disclosure, Taylor is a friend and an important source for my book, *The Killing of Karen Silkwood*. He was the lead investigator in the Silkwood family's negligence lawsuit against Karen Silkwood's employer, the Kerr-McGee Nuclear Corporation. Furthermore, Taylor and the second criminal investigator, Gail H. Johnson, are friends and colleagues.

Both investigators are so convinced of their conclusions that they put their reputations on the line and gave me permission to reveal their names. Johnson also made it clear that he had not discussed the Rudnitski case with Taylor before I interviewed him. The third criminal investigator requested to remain anonymous. The purpose of three interviews was to see if the criminal investigators agreed with Dr. Baker's suicide ruling without knowing about Brother Alphonse.

All three investigators independently agreed that the death of Kenneth Rudnitski was a suspicious death that called for an autopsy.

All three agreed that Kenneth was murdered. They based their conclusion on the fact that the Red's death clearly appeared to be staged and that there was no sign of a struggle. In most, but not all suicides, the body struggles in extremis as it becomes air-starved.

In the case of Red, not only were there no signs of struggle, such as bruised feet or elbows from pounding against the stall partition and the floor. In fact, his feet were perfectly aligned. All three concluded that Red may have been killed somewhere other than in the stall, and that his body was planted in the stall to make his death appear to be suicide.

Johnson attached a 90 percent probability to his conclusion that Red was murdered, leaving ten percent to the unlikelihood that Red may have hung himself, passed out, and died without moving. Both Taylor and the anonymous investigator were 100 percent certain of their homicide conclusions.

The homicide conclusion of the three criminal investigators is supported by a string of interconnected and weighty circumstantial evidence. Brother Alphonse was the last known person to see Red alive. That makes him a prime suspect. The timeline supports homicide. Ed Harte interrupted Brother Alphonse's late-night attack on Red. Brother Alphonse ran out of the dormitory right behind Red. Dr. Baker placed Kenneth Rudnitski's death at around midnight. Brother Alphonse hid.

Brother Alphonse had motive, opportunity, and means to kill Red. He wouldn't want his superiors to know he was attacking boys in the school. He had to keep Red from talking. So he chased, caught Red, threatened to kill Red if he talked, and then let him go. Or Alphonse tried to prevent Red from yelling out. In trying to subdue him, Brother Alphonse either deliberately or accidentally murdered Red.

Besides opportunity, Brother Alphonse had the means to kill Red—his hands and arms. As a World War II veteran, Peter Horne learned how to use the choke hold to either subdue or kill someone.

Finally, Brother Alphonse ran and hid for several days during freezing March weather. Why would he hide like a guilty person if Red had committed suicide? It would be mission accomplished. Suicide would have silenced Red as definitively as homicide. With suicide, there wasn't a shred of evidence to implicate Brother Alphonse without an autopsy.

***

I find that the preponderance of circumstantial evidence points to homicide. I conclude that Brother Alphonse Horne murdered Kenny "Red" Rudnitski late night on March 8, 1960.

JUSTICE FOR RED

The State of Wisconsin was negligent in its one-day investigation into the death of Kenneth "Red" Rudnitski. Justice demands the Wisconsin State Attorney General order a re-examination of the boy's death. Justice also demands that the State order an exhumation, and that the skeleton of Kennth Rudnitski be examined by a forensic pathologist.

AFTERWORD

Sheriff Joseph Dorr died in 1965.

Dr. Ross Baker died in 1984.

Father Charles Malin died in 1983.

Paul Jacobi resigned from the priesthood and died in 1990.

Brother Alphonse Horne died in 1991.

Detective Werner Voegeli died in 1998.

Father John McHenry died in 2011.

Divine Word Seminary was demolished in 1993.

Between 1937, when it opened its doors, and 1993 when it closed them, 1,962 boys studied there.

***

Bill Burrows discussed the death of Kenny Rudnitski with Mr. Jacobi and Father McHenry many years after Red's death. Both men had good recall on everything but Red's death. They said they remembered "little about the suicide."

ACKNOWLEDGMENTS

I would like to thank:

Patrick Leddy for introducing me to the Kenneth "Red" Rudnitski story. Dick Hahner for helping to find former East Troy students, locating the documents which became the foundation for Red's story, granting permission to publish his poem, for his research and guidance. Bud May for help in the investigation in and around East Troy and Elkhorn and for sharing photos. Bill Burrows for critiquing drafts of the book and providing insight, direction, and guidance. Duane Dargis, Michaela Meehan, and Aina Stunz for critiquing drafts and editing. Guy Rashke and Dan Rashke for critiquing an early draft.

Attorneys Helen McGonigle and Bruce Rashke for advice on the legal issues and critiquing drafts. Forensic Pathologist Dr. Joseph Hodge for reviewing all matters medical, advising me, and critiquing a draft; criminal investigators William J. Taylor and Gail H. Johnson for their evaluations and conclusions on the death of Kenneth "Red" Rudnitski. Gavin DeWulf for proofreading. Gina Carver, lead investigator on the Walworth County Medical Examiner's team and the Walworth County Historical Society.

Gavin DeWulf, Gabrielle Henman, Kristen LePine, Helen McGonigle, Doug Moe, Barbara Rashke, Bruce Rashke, Dan Rashke, and Scribeworks for their help with marketing and promotion.

CHAPTER END NOTES

THE NARRATIVE

Paradise Lost

History of Holy Ghost Mission House: Peklo, Father Edward. *The East Troy Story, 1921-2012.* Printed privately, 7-11.

February 1960

Anne Veronica Burns Fitzgerald: McCahill, Ed. "The Liberation of Tim Fitzgerald: One Man's March from Rogers Park to Lincoln Park." *Chicago Magazine,* August 1978.

Tuesday March 8th—Mid-Morning

U.S Public Health Report, *Suicides in the United States 1930-1965;* also "1960 Arrests Low in Walworth County." *Janesville Daily Gazette*, March 4, 1961.

Reasons for not reporting: "Statistics About Sexual Violence." National Sex Violence Resource Center.

1 in 6 under reported: Ibid. Also Brown, Emma. "A Silent Crisis." *Washington Post Magazine*, February 28, 2021.

12 percent: National Sex Violence Resource Center.

"Taking things too seriously..." Brown.

"Some boys don't even..." Ibid.

Voegeli: Inscription on his gravestone in Mount Pleasant Cemetery, Tibits, Wisconsin reads: "1st Lieutenant US Army...World War II...05/14/1922-09/22/1998." Also Dick Hahner's interview with Voegeli's daughter Lynn Grooms.

Voegeli citation: "Motion Under Rule Seven, The State of Wisconsin, Citation by Legislature."

Dorr: "Dorr Paid High Tribute on Retirement After 41 Years as Law Officer." *Janesville Daily Gazette*, May 1, 1962; also obituary, April 17, 1962.

Tuesday March 8th—Mid-Afternoon

"Janesville Seminarian Hangs Self..." *Janesville Daily Gazette*, March 8, 1960; also obituary, March 11, 1960.

Leo I. Brust: *Fond Du Lac Reporter* obituary, February 2, 1995; *Kenosha News* obituary, February 2, 1995.

Mid-March 1960

The other three students on the morale committee were: Bill Burrows (Junior). Jim Bergin (Senior), and Beemer Riley (Senior).

ANALYSIS

The Making of Alphonse Horne

Registration card: D. S. S. Form 1, order number 609.

South Pacific: *Augusta Chronicle*, November 2, 1944.

Welch Rehabilitation Hospital: *Augusta Chronicle*, November 2, 1944. Watkins, John G. "Hypnosis: Seventy Years of Amazement and Still Don't Know What it is." *Journal of Clinical Hypnosis*, 52:2, October 2009; O'Keefe, Daniel E. "Zone of Interior." *Neuropsychiatry World War Two*, volume one. U.S. Army Medical Department, Office of Medical History.

"Who lost their capacity..." O'Keefe, 621.

"Mild psychoneuroses..." Ibid.

Half of the soldiers: Watkins, 135.

Admissions Card: National Archives (NARA) Hospital Admission Card Files, Records of the Office of the Surgeon General (Army), 1775-1994, Record Group 112.

Astigmatism: Ellis, Michael. "Four Eyes: Eyeglasses and the World War II GI"; "Physical Standards in World War II: Army Medical Corps 1967." *National Library of Medicine*, Bethesda, Maryland; also *Numbers Game@90thIDPG.us*. U.S. Department of Health, 1967.

Bay St. Louis: Meier, Rev. Michael, S.V.D. *Divine Word Missionaries Black Apostolate*. Rome: Pontifica Universitas Gregoriana, 1959. (Dissertation).

The Misfit

Crossing sexual boundaries: Coleman, Gerald D. "Clergy Sexual Abuse and Homosexuality." Plante, Thomas G. *Sin Against the Innocents: Sexual Abuse by Priests and the Role of the Catholic Church.* Thomas Plante, Editor. Westport, CT: Praeger, 2004, 74.

Characteristics: Markham, Donna J, and Mikail, Samuel F. "Perpetrators of Clergy Abuse of Minors: Insights from Attachment Theory." Plante, 102.

The Parting of the Veil

"We are making…" Herguth, Robert. "Cardinal Blasé Cupich Demanding Details About Order Priests But Won't Post Findings," February 5, 2021.

"Exporting Abusive Priests…" Herguth, Robert. "Exporting Abusive Priests: Catholic Religious Order Based Near Northbrook Reveals Abusers." *Chicago Sun-Times*, May 14, 2021; and Esposito, Stephan. "Attorney Wants Full List of Problem Religious Order Priests in State Made Public." *The Chicago Sun Times*, June 4, 2021.

"The List," is a composite of three separate lists: Southern Province, Western Province, and Chicago Province.

Joseph Fertal: "Fr. Joseph Fertal—Diocese of San Bernardino," August 21, 2020, *The Sun*, February 5 and May 14.

The Shuffle and the Shelf

Gay Priests: Part of my research was to tally the number of gay priests and brothers at Divine Word College in Washington, D.C. The number came to slightly more than half. As part of my research, and since I am not gay, I visited gay bars with gay priests. Jacques Nyssen was one of the priests who was my gay-bar guide.

According to The List, the pedophiles and/or sexual predators working in Ghana besides Nyssen, were: Fathers Ronald Lange, Vance Thorne, Michael Carew, and Brother Henry Miller.

According to The List, the pedophiles and/or sexual predators living at Divine Word College besides Nyssen, Alphonse, and Camillus were: Brothers Anthony Hogan and Arthur Kelly.

The Boy Who Knew Too Much

Fitzgerald background: McCahil, Ed. "The Liberation of Tim Fitzgerald: One Man's Long March from Rogers Park to Lincoln Park." *Chicago Magazine*, August 1978.

Fitzgerald's conviction: State of Michigan, Second Circuit Court Case No: 2017000374 and 2017000374-FH. Also: "Bottled Blonde Attorney Jailed on Drug Charges, Delayed Final Hearing," *dna.com/chicago*, updated September 20, 2017. Glastris, Paul. "Second City Son." *U.S. News and World Report*, April 15, 1991.

Assault and battery: "Attorney Timothy Fitzgerald of Chicago, Convicted of Assault." *Neoethics.Net/news* (undated).

The Boy Who Saw Too Much

Marmion Academy: *privateschoolreview.com/marmionacademy*.

The Four Hartes: Ed Harte, Greg Laka, Bob Kairis, and Ron Barrett. Ron Barrett is dead.

Filling Holes/Mission Impossible

Brandewie, *In the Light of the Word: Divine Word Missionaries of North America*. New York: Orbis Books, 2000, p.135. *CARA Report*, 107, 1975. Quoted by Brandewie, 104-105.

Dr. Ross Baker—The Elephant in the Room

"In Memoriam: Dr. Ross B. Baker." *East Troy Times*, March 17, 2005.

Gymnasium fire: Peklo, 21.

Dedication brochure: *Dedication of the Chapel. School Addition and Gymnasium of Holy Ghost Mission Seminary on September 28. 1952.*

Kaufman, Christopher. *Faith and Fraternalism: The History of the Knights of Columbus 1882-1992*. New York: Harper and Row, 1982, 276-277.

"Or some other suitable…" 1989 *Charter*, Section 125.

Sheriff Joseph Dorr—Man of Mystery

Seminary priests served at St. Peter's Catholic Church: Peklo, 11. It is unclear when seminary priests began serving as chaplains.

Zero murders/ten suicides: "1960 Arrests at 8-Year Low," *Janesville Daily Gazette*, March 4, 1961.

"We all know…" "Dorr Paid High Tribute on Retirement After 41 Years as a Law Officer." *Janesville Daily Gazette*, May 1, 1962.

Walworth County

Microfilming coroner's reports: Author's 2020 interview with Gina Carver, chief investigator at the current Walworth County Medical Examiner's Office.

Suicide

CDC Guidelines: "Criteria for Determining Suicide," December 23, 1988.

ABOUT THE AUTHOR

RICHARD RASHKE is the author of several controversial nonfiction books, including *The Killing of Karen Silkwood*, *Escape From Sobibor*, and *Useful Enemies*. His books and plays have been translated into thirteen languages and have been the subject of movies for screen and television. His award-winning play, *Dear Esther*, has been produced every year since its premiere at the United States Holocaust Memorial Museum in 1998. It was performed in Polish in the "Sobibor Musem" at the Sobibor death camp site in Poland in 2023.

RED RABBIT BOOKS

RedRabbit-Books.com